KATE & DAVID,

Hope you Dig the recipes!

Happy COOKIN'

Best wishes

AUG '17

JUNK FOOD JAPAN

week, and I'd have to give up the next level of high school. I could live with the quitting high school part, but one thing I did realise I'd be giving up was my, at the time, passion - running. I couldn't manage the long kitchen hours and train like I'd been used to, and so, sadly, running fell by the wayside.

So, I got signed up as an apprentice chef; I had the full chef whites, including a neckerchief, and I bought my first proper knife, which cost me my first week's pay; I think I still have it somewhere.

My first chef was a Frenchman, a mad one as well. I remember the entire team, aside from us apprentices, were European - it was some serious shit. I can't imagine it being as strict and focused there these days; the cost of putting that team together would kill it for starters. My first section was to prep the cold buffet every morning from 7am. The chef was always in early which meant the pressure was always on, so when he disappeared to play tennis with the maître d' from the fine dining outlet on certain afternoons we could breathe easy for an hour!… Or so I thought.

One day he came racing in, in his full tennis gear, came right up to me and said 'Monsieur, I heard you got a tennis racquet for Christmas'. I nervously replied with 'Ahhhh, yes chef?!' 'Right, well get on your bike, ride home and get it. Norbert is sick today, so you're playing me now.' FUCK! I didn't know my ass from my elbow when it came to tennis, but I tried to hit the ball, missed a load of times and the chef then threw a John McEnroe and ended up walking off the court. Pure madness, but one of my favourite memories from my five years at the hotel.

So, life as an apprentice became pretty sweet. I'd moved into a flat with a couple of guys from the hotel - which I was kicked out of about six months later. Pool parties and drum practice aren't just frowned upon; the fellow residents fucking hated it. At this stage my mum was freaking out, I was still only 16 years old. I moved in with a fellow apprentice known as Mung Bean; my mum thought he was such a nice sensible young man - good job, Bean! Little did she know he was as nuts as the rest of us! He did, however, begin to instill a certain level of professionalism in me. Yeah, ok, he was the sensible one.

It was guys like Munga (aka Dave Allen), Mike Brown (aka Brownie, Brown Francis or Morton) and Dave the 'Lang Monster' Lang, who were not only a few years older than me but were also highly competitive and dedicated professionals of the industry, who had a positive influence. They encouraged me to enter apprentice chef cooking contests, which I won a few medals at - even at national level. These guys were proud of our profession and I loved the way they worked hard and played hard. So, on a good day I was winning cooking contests; on an even better day I was stealing rowing boats with Lang (Dave, the coastguard didn't get your message, that boat is still drifting, dude!).

Eventually I got itchy feet and moved to the (bigger) city of Perth, and that was cool; food was hip and things were OK, but it didn't cut it for me. I hooked up with Morton, who'd just returned from a season in Chamonix and we drove around Australia in his legendary Subaru. It was 1997 and that (sadly) was the last time I would live in my home state. I hopped off the road trip in North Queensland and landed a job on the amazing Hayman Island. What an experience this was - I started to learn about a proper Asian kitchen; how to work the woks, make various dumplings, make sauces and dressings that I'd never heard of, and attempt to make sushi - in hindsight the sushi was a total joke.

I had to more or less teach myself - I bought a book and got to it. I'd love to see photos of what I came up with; I imagine it looked pretty, down to my roulade making, *chaud froid* platter-decorating days of the cold buffet back in Bunbury, but I bet it tasted like total shit!

As great as it was, snorkling the Great Barrier Reef on days off, playing guitar at open mic nights in the staff bar whilst Metallica loomed in the corner (I didn't have a clue they were watching), it was time to keep moving. I'd met a girl from Melbourne on the island, Peri, and we decided to travel to Canada together. We ended up in Toronto which had a really buzzing food scene. I got stuck into my job for about eight months before getting a call from a Swiss chef, Martin Z'graggen, who asked me to join his team in Zermatt, Switzerland, to help open a funky new hotel. It didn't take much arm twisting!

Solo, I left for the Alps to be the saucier, eventually in both of the hotel restaurants. Not an easy feat when the service is called in German. (It really is amazing how fast you can pick up language if you need to.) Fellow chefs would also help me with it after service by teaching me to offend bar staff at our local. We were kicked out of that joint for less than we should have been!

Anyway, that winter season ended and I went back to Western Australia for a few months and cooked with Mung Bean. I had no idea what I'd do next, I only knew I had no money and I hated cooking well done steaks for drunken bogans. To my rescue came a call from Mike Brown - 'we're gonna open a restaurant in Chamonix; get your ass over here!' I didn't really give a fuck about the hows or whys, I just took off.

I'm still not sure if this move was partly naïve, stupid or even brave: I suspect a bit of each. Mike and I could cook pretty well but we didn't really know shit about the complex ride of a restaurateur.

Mega ass kicking #1: we had to renovate an old fondue restaurant, which stank of decades of rancid raclette, but this was the least of our problems. We were two mid-twenty something kids from the south west of Western Australia in Chamonix, with little clue about how it was all supposed to work, including staff laws, tax and how to get around or, should I say, pay off individuals where necessary. However, with a little help of a borrowed Volvo, a hard-working Danish couple (Mike is now happily married to one of them - Marie, not Simon), we won the battle!

We worked so fucking hard cooking up Thai green curry of rabbit (which confused the fuck out of the locals at first) and an ever-changing menu of other killer pan-Asian dishes, that snowboarding was a total afterthought. I recall Mike and I had a Sunday off so we went up the mountain to have a day of boarding, did one run and packed it in exhausted! We ended up lying on his bed watching a movie with kebab. I'm sure Mike's girlfriend at the time thought I'd muscled in on her man; it must have looked hilarious when she rocked up. It was the only TV in the house though!

So, the Chamonix adventure came to an end and London was calling! Peri was living there after she had left Canada and I was in need of a favour. I had zero cash, a maxed out credit card, which I'm pleased to say still worked from time to time, and a half paid for mountain bike. Peri had bought me a flight out of Geneva but that was a fair hike from Chamonix. Thanks to a popular rental car company, who kind of loaned me a vehicle, I was on my way! The trouble was, that particular vehicle didn't have the correct tax sticker for me to drive it into Switzerland. I was told by the girls with guns at the border that I could purchase the correct sticker and be on my way. My trusty credit card could do the job perhaps? Wrong! I was stuck. My plane was leaving in a few hours and I couldn't go back with the rental car or I'd have to pay - what to do?

Things became a little overwhelming at that point and a tear or two might have popped out. I really had no idea which way to turn. Luckily, one of the heavily armed Swiss girls guarding the border (not to criticise, but not guarding it too well on this occasion), came up close and whispered 'Just go! Drive to the east and go into Switzerland'. More tears, a massive hug and I was fucking outta there. After stashing the rental car right out the front of Geneva airport I raced to the check in desk and secured my seat on board the plane - outta there, finally!

I landed in London and made my way to Peri's place in Bayswater. She and her twenty-odd housemates offered me a lovely place under the staircase to sleep. Peri told me, 'I'm leaving for Singapore on a conference tomorrow - I'll be back in a week, get your shit together.' And, to everyone's surprise, that's exactly what I did!

Within days I was working at the amazing Nobu as a chef de partie. Slowly I started to really fall in love with Nobu's vibrant, innovative and highly credible take on Japanese cuisine. I loved it so much, I knew for sure that Japanese cuisine would be in my heart and soul forever - so far, I have to say, I was pretty fucking spot on!

I could tell you a thousand stories about my six years at Nobu Park Lane, or the year I spent opening Nobu Melbourne, but that is a whole other story and I'd need another 300 pages - not to mention how slowly I churn out my writing! I will say this though, Nobu was a thrilling ride that schooled my ass in Japanese cuisine and culture. Once I'd worked up to the Head Chef role I was in a position whereby I could learn how large teams work, how to manage exclusive events, how to behave around mega stars and sometimes my rock star idols, but, most of all, how to cook in a Japanese style with passion. We constantly excited our guests; there was no greater pleasure than to see folks genuinely loving our food.

I started to become creative with the sauces and ingredients at Nobu. I even set up a specials section as an outlet for not only mine but the other chefs specials to be focused on with the commitment that these new dishes required. But, after a time, there is only so much you can create under somebody else's name, so I was off again!

I fiddled around with a few projects in Dubai, Bahrain and eventually a little town in West Sussex called Horsham. But the trouble was I seemed to be trying to do a kind of Nobu replica; it wasn't what I'd describe as my own thing, it was what other ex-Nobu chefs did. In hindsight it was crap idea - don't get me wrong, we did some great food, but the overall offering was a bit full of shit. Fast forward two years into this project and I was sick of my bullshit business partners. I had to do something for myself. I wasn't happy serving my food in an environment steered by others. I had to have full control if there was ever going to be a well rounded offering that I believed in. If I could create this it would be rock 'n' roll, great food without being pretentious and it would be staffed by shiny, happy people.

I'm not too sure how many people believed in the whole idea at first. I sat in my garage writing out my plans and menus, studying restaurant designs, researching average spends etc. Everything went on a wall chart and I constantly scrutinised it all, often ripping it down and starting again.

Eventually I hooked up with one of my current business partners, Andrew Stafford, who I'd worked at Nobu with. Andrew was Nobu's Financial Controller back in the day, and just the right person to sit and talk plans, especially numbers, over a thousand beers!

We eventually attracted funding and found our first site - that was a 'Holy Shit' kind of moment. Suddenly this wasn't just a bunch of ideas on my shed wall - this fucker was becoming real! So we get stuck into the design and build; the money was coming in on time and we had a fairly good idea of our launch date - too easy!

Wrong! Our next round of funds was running late, really fucking late. Our investor had gone quiet and we didn't have much dosh left in the bank. So far we had only employed one person, a mate of mine, Mark Morrans, who had worked for me as a chef since my days at Nobu Melbourne. (I might add that at this point in time, Mark was homeless and living in the building site on a fold up camp bed - or at times the toilet floor!)

I had asked Mark to look for a pop-up space to launch Kurobuta - we had building costs to cover and a launch date to hit; a pop up was the only way we could make it all happen, and that's only if this thing would actually take off.

Mark came across this little joint on the King's Road in Chelsea - an ex-piano shop which had been partially converted into a restaurant site. The kitchen was at domestic level at best; the tables and chairs could have been mistaken for collapsible; there was zero storage and the basement was prone to flooding - and often!

I recall pacing up and down a hotel room in Jeddah, Saudi Arabia, where I'd gone to earn a little cash in the uncertain meantime. If we decided to jump into the deep end and take on the King's Road pop-up we stood the chance of fucking it all up - and really quickly too! We could use up all of our cash and blow our chance of building the Kurobuta brand.

I was trying to weigh up the pros and cons but I didn't want to really think about it like that. After about 200 metres of pacing in my little hotel room I thought, fuck it, let's jump in head first and smash it - and that's exactly what we did.

We had four and a half days from me landing back in London and picking up the keys to fix up the restaurant and open on the Friday night to friends and family. The next day at 12pm was the real deal - we opened up to the public and knocked out around 100 covers. It works, it fucking works!!

Kurobuta was brought to life; it wasn't just alive, it was firing on all cylinders and blowing people away. The place was a happy shambles, the chairs would break, the fruit and veg stored on the shelves would fall on our guests' heads, staff would fall down the stairs and we were so packed out we struggled to get through the tiny gaps between tables; delivering the food was like playing pass the parcel. I'd never felt so proud.

Three years later and large portions of blood, sweat and tears, I present you with an insight into Kurobuta and the way I love to approach my food, life and business.

As my old pop would say, right before we sat down to family meals, 'Get stuck into it and sleep on bags.'

Scott Hallsworth
London, 2017

SNACK

CRUNCHY CHICKEN SKIN WITH POTATO-TRUFFLE DIP

Who can resist crunchy, salty chicken skin? Even those who don't eat meat have been known to salivate when they smell these fresh out of the oven. It's only natural right? We were born with umami receptors on our palettes, and those of us who were breastfed were getting hooked on it from day one - kind of explains our addiction to tastiness!

Ask your butcher for chicken skins (this sort of implies that we all have our very own butcher, some might but for those who don't and are here with me in 2017, ask someone at the meat counter in your supermarket). Anyway, chicken skins are readily available, especially with a little bit of notice - make sure your butler lets your butcher know.

MAKES ENOUGH FOR THE FIRST 10 MINUTES OF A FOOTBALL MATCH IF 2 PEOPLE ARE WATCHING

1kg chicken skins, washed and
    drained well
sea salt

For the potato-truffle dip
200g cold mashed potatoes
50g Greek yoghurt
35ml lemon juice
2 teaspoons yuzu juice
white truffle oil, to taste (you could grate
    fresh truffle over if you want to
    get fancy)
a pinch of flaked sea salt
a pinch of sansho pepper

Crank the oven to 180°C/160°C fan/Gas Mark 4.

On a silicon mat or baking sheet, evenly spread the skins out so that they are flat. They can be quite close together as they shrink loads. (You might need to use multiple trays or cook the skins in batches, depending on your oven size.) Sprinkle generously with salt.

Roast in the oven for about 30 minutes. They are ready when they have turned golden and become irresistibly crunchy.

To make the dip, fold all the ingredients together, using a spatula.

Allow the skins to cool to room temperature and just before serving simply sprinkle them with a little sea salt and serve with the dip on the side.

BROAD BEAN TEMPURA WITH WASABI SALT

Broad beans are in fact fairly common in Japan, in season of course. This is one of the two things I love to do with them when spring comes around. The other is grilling them on our robata grill in the pods. They are the ultimate bar snack – serve them with salt and a wet wipe.

I use our extra-crunchy trisol tempura batter for this, as it stays crunchy longer than other versions of tempura. The wasabi salt works with other tempura, too.

MAKES A SMALL SNACK FOR 2

8 broad bean pods
1 litre rapeseed oil, for deep-frying
tempura flour, for lightly coating
60ml trisol batter (see page 251)
lemon wedges, to serve

For the wasabi salt

50g flaked sea salt (such as Maldon)
10g wasabi powder, mixed with a little
   water to form a paste (if you're lucky
   enough to have fresh wasabi and a
   shark skin grater then yee-ha, add
   enough to taste)

It's ideal if you make the wasabi salt a few days ahead, as the salt takes on the wasabi flavour far better. Simply mix the salt and the wasabi paste. This salt must be kept covered so that it stays almost moist and for that reason you need to keep it refrigerated. It will clump when you do this so as you go to sprinkle it, give it a grind between your fingers and thumb to break it up a little. (This recipe makes more than you need, but keep it in the fridge for use with other tempura.)

First remove the beans from the pod and pick away at the thin skin surrounding each broad bean. (I know this is a total pain in the ass, but it's essential.)

Heat the oil in a fryer or large pan to 180°C/350°F.

Lightly coat the beans in the tempura flour and shake off any excess. Dip them in the trisol batter and drop into the hot, pristine rapeseed oil.

Allow them to become golden, unlike classic tempura. It should take about 2 minutes. Remove from the oil with a perforated scoop and set on kitchen paper to drain. Sprinkle with the salt and serve with lemon wedges for squeezing.

FLAMED EDAMAME WITH BUTTER, LEMON AND SEA SALT

Ever tried these little buggers? Of course you have. You'll no doubt remember them as boiled (usually in dirty pots of overused water that sometimes chefs don't or won't change during service, yuck!) and salted pods of pale green young soybeans, and if you've seen them advertised as steamed then carry on dreaming – every joint I know that claims this is lying. Why? Steamed reads far better than boiled. You may have been assaulted with the spicy ones too – not for me – in this case they are often just tossed in store-bought chilli paste, or, even worse, soaked in the crap!

I have to mention one last thing. When you tuck into edamame you're meant to nibble the outer pod so as to pop the two or three little edamame out – eat the inner part only and toss the outer skin. Ok, it might sound obvious but I will now tell you why I'm bothering to include instructions.

So, a few years back I was dining with my at-the-time backers. They really didn't know shit from clay and on this occasion we were dining a very dynamic, well-dined and very intelligent business man from New York. One of the nouveau-riche backers began to complain – in full earshot of us all – that this serving of edamame contained absolutely no beans inside at all – however they tasted great. Boom! This guy had been eating out of the scrap bowl, which contained everyone else's chewed up skins, complete with all of our saliva, germs and whatever else we contributed to his 'tasty' treats.

As for my version, I scorch the skins after tossing the fuckers in sake and butter. I use a wood oven but before we could afford one we used an old wok and buried it amongst a shitload of hot coals so that it got scorching hot. Here's what we do...

SERVES 1 AS PART OF A MULTI-COURSE MENU, AND CAN EASILY BE SCALED UP

a handful of defrosted edamame per
person (an average-sized hand, not
Michael Jackson's, who, when I shook
his giant mit, shook half my arm
as well!)
40ml melted clarified butter, really warm
30ml sake – keep it classy, Junmai
Daiginjo stylie
Maldon sea salt, to season
lemon wedges, to serve

Toss the edamame, butter and sake together and whack into your wood/pizza oven – a home oven won't do!

If you don't have a wood oven, your best choice now is to heat up an old pan so that it has the potential to set off your neighbour's smoke alarm – send a warning to air traffic control, this shit kicks off.

Now slap the edamame into the pan and shake it like a whole fistful of Polaroid pictures! Colour it up and tip it right into your serving bowl – juices and all.

Sprinkle with Maldon sea salt or some other fancy bullshit salt, which isn't as good. Be generous with the salt. Serve with a lemon wedge and an empty bowl so that total dickheads can eat your scraps!

CRUNCHY RICE SENBEI IN AVOCADO-JALAPEÑO DIP

This is one of the first snacks that we served at Kurobuta. Senbei is fairly easy to make and if you stay ahead with the drying process you can have fresh, crunchy senbei in minutes.

I often press sesame seeds into the sheets before drying but you can also add things like shredded nori or boiled soba grains, or even flavour the mixture before spreading with shichimi togarashi or even saffron (which goes well with the spicy tuna maki, see page 134).

SERVES 2

Senbei mix (see page 33), but omit
   the saffron
1 litre rapeseed oil, for deep-frying

For the avocado-jalapeño dip

1 avocado, peeled, destoned and flesh
   finely diced
½ blindingly hot jalapeño chilli, chopped
   with seeds and membrane
20ml spicy Korean miso (see page 249)
1 tablespoon yuzu juice
2 teaspoons lemon juice
sea salt and freshly ground black pepper

To serve

1 teaspoon spicy Korean miso (see
   page 249)
chopped chives, optional
white sesame seeds or coriander
   leaves, optional

Prepare the crunchy senbei as directed on page 33. Spread the sheets out on a non-stick silicon mat (or baking sheet lined with baking parchment) about 2.5mm thick. (Use a wet angled palate knife for best results.) I dehydrate the sheets but you can put in a low oven (about 110°C/90°C fan/Gas Mark ¼) for 8–12 hours or so, until thoroughly dried. It will look hard and translucent, a bit like a sheet of plastic. Remove and let cool, after which you can store the rice sheets in an airtight container. Or start to puff them…

To puff the senbei, heat the oil in a fryer or large pan to 210–220°C/410–425°F (it has to be clean, fresh oil – if it's been used before bits of sediment will burn immediately and you'll end up with a burnt taste on your crackers).

Break the senbei into small pieces – they will double in size so have this in mind – then drop the pieces into the hot oil one at a time, they will puff immediately. Pull them out with a perforated scoop and rest on kitchen paper. Repeat until you finish frying however much senbei you need. Cook only what you need – it's best to fry up senbei and eat them fresh.

Quickly make the dip by putting on a disposable glove and squishing the ingredients together – you want the ingredients to bind without ending up with something too smooth.

Break the senbei into roughly 3–4cm × 3–4cm pieces. Place a heaped teaspoon of the dip on top of a double bite-sized piece of senbei. Drizzle with a little spicy Korean miso. Garnish with chopped chives and sesame seeds if you like – coriander is good, too.

FRIED CASHEWS WITH DRIED MISO, LIME AND CHILLI

I say this about most spicy, moreish snacks, but these are the best ever! I have a long list of 'best ever' bar snacks - nuts are the most obvious or most basic, but done well, as you'll all probably know, they are pure addiction. I've tossed this version in a Japanese syrup called kuromitsu. It's basically a black sugar syrup, most often used for pouring over vanilla ice cream (it's so damn good).

I boost the umami factor by making some dried miso powder. It's also great for sprinkling over salads or sashimi, or to use as a replacement for salt.

SERVES 2

16g miso powder (see method for how to make this from miso paste)
1 litre rapeseed oil, for deep-frying
50g cashews
80g demerara sugar
1 dried red chilli, roughly crumbled
1 lime

Preheat the oven to its lowest setting, or around 110°C/90°C fan/Gas Mark ¼. Spread some miso paste thinly onto a silicon mat or baking sheet and allow to dry in your oven. (Alternatively, your best bet is to use a dehydrator if you have one.) When dried thoroughly, grind until you have a fine powder and set aside until ready to use.

Heat the oil in a fryer or large pan to 180°/350°F, and deep-fry the cashews until golden, around 2 minutes. Remove with a perforated spoon and drain well on kitchen paper.

Line a tray with baking paper or have ready a silicon mat. Heat the sugar in a pan over a medium-high heat, until it turns to liquid and colours slightly as it comes up to the boil. Toss in the fried cashews, dried chilli, zest and juice of half a lime. Cook for 20 seconds and tip onto the silicon mat or baking paper-lined tray. Sprinkle evenly with the dried miso and allow to cool, and then break up into pieces.

Serve with half a lime on the side – it might seem odd to serve lime on nuts, but it helps counteract the heat from the chilli. Eat now! (Or store in an airtight container.)

SWEET POTATO AND SOBA KO FRIES

I used to make these at home for my kids, and no matter how imperfect I thought they were, the kids still loved them. It was a case of not quite getting the crunch I wanted without getting too much colour: very slightly too much colour equals burnt for my kids. 'Overly browned food' is the one thing I can't get them to eat.

The trick with these fries is to give them the old double-cooked treatment. First at a low temperature to soften them up, and then at a higher temperature to quickly give them a good ole crunching!

I tried to coat them with tempura batter as well as plain flour, but it wasn't 100 per cent and they were slightly chewy. Soba flour sprang to mind because of its lack of gluten. Firstly, I prefer to avoid gluten where possible (well, at least I plan to!), and secondly it makes for a 'shorter' kind of crunch. Plus, it tastes pretty fecking good!

MAKES 1 PORTION TO SHARE OR NOT TO SHARE

1 litre rapeseed oil, for deep-frying
200g sweet potato, peeled and cut into really thin, long chips
60g soba (buckwheat) flour
30ml spicy Korean miso (see page 249)

For the spicy seasoning mix
3 teaspoons Maldon sea salt
2 teaspoons shichimi togarashi
a small pinch of hot dashi powder

For the green chilli dressing (it will make more than you need, but keep it in the fridge for another time)
100g green chillies (take a slice from the fat end first to see how fiery they are; if they're too hot for you, then remove the membrance and seeds)
100ml rice vinegar
120ml grapeseed oil
a pinch of sea salt

To serve – all optional but the more the merrier I say!
chopped green chillies
2–3 lime wedges

First make the green chilli dressing. Chop the chillies into small pieces and combine with the rice vinegar and a pinch of salt. Blend on a high speed until the chillies have broken down. With the motor still running, slowly trickle the grapeseed oil into the blended chilli mix until it has been fully incorporated. Stop the blender immediately, pour the mixture through a fine strainer and keep in the fridge until you need it.

Heat the oil in a fryer or large pan to 140°C/275°F. For the first round of frying, fry the sweet potato for about 4–5 minutes, until soft and kind of soggy looking.

Remove from the oil with a perforated scoop and allow to drain well. Be careful as you move them, as they'll be fragile at this stage.

Increase the temperature of the oil to 180°C/350°F. Put your soggy chips into a bowl and pour over the soba flour and about 2 tablespoons of water. Mix well – gently but thoroughly.

Place these into the oil one at a time and fry for 2–3 minutes, until crunchy, and then remove with a perforated spoon and allow to drain.

To finish off, quickly smash all the spicy seasoning mix together in a mortar and pestle or the Japanese (and far superior) version, the suribachi. Season your hot fries with 10 big pinches of the spicy seasoning mix and serve up with the chillies, lime and dressing on the side. Get 'em while they're hot!

CRAB `STICKS´

To most of us, the name 'crab sticks' conjures up thoughts of that overly sweet, sturdy, red-dyed shit that is all too often passed off as crab, or crab sticks (surimi).

When I moved to Dubai, I was told that we had to serve crab sticks (or as we called it, crab-shit) because the locals loved the stuff. Jeez, how true that was! We had requests for side orders of the shit, shredded up and tossed in spicy mayo, and we served up over 1,200 litre buckets with one shovel per person. The first to slip into a crab coma probably won something. I can't see why else they would do it, it's fucking gross. Anyway, in protest, no, maybe more of a piss-take, I decided

to make my own (edible) crab sticks. Crunchy little fuckers, made with real crab and confusing as hell to this lot - 'what, I can't believe it's not full of deadly shit that's gonna kill me' - arrrgggghhh!

You could argue that surimi are widely used in Japan - sure they are, but does that automatically qualify them as decent Japanese restaurant fodder - fuck no.

Go make an effort and buy or catch some real crab - it's one of my favourite shellfish and it's all natural.

This recipe is easy peasy, you just need to be slightly patient.

MAKES SHIT-LOADS OF THE CRUNCHY-CAN'T-FUCKING-STOP-EATING-THEM CRAB STICKS

100g senbei mix (see page 33)

30g brown crabmeat

45g white crabmeat (I usually use king crab)

a generous pinch of katsuobushi (bonito flakes)

1 teaspoon la-yu (spicy sesame oil)

1 teaspoon light soy sauce

a large pinch of Maldon sea salt

a few grinds of black pepper

1 litre rapeseed oil, for deep-frying

yuzu kosho mayo (see page 252), to serve

Purée all the ingredients except the oil and mayo in a food processor until smooth, and then chill for 20 minutes.

You need to cut a very small piece from the tip of a very small piping bag so that you just end up piping a line approximately 5mm wide.

Half-fill the piping bag (so that it's easily managed) with the chilled crab mix. Pipe 15cm lengths onto some baking parchment or, better still, a silicon mat.

Best drying method: dehydrate on full power for 4 hours.
Second-best method: dry in a super-low oven, around 110°C/90°C fan/Gas Mark ¼, or its lowest setting. A hot room would do it if you don't mind waiting for a day and a half.

Once the sticks are as hard as a piece of plastic they are done. You can store them in the fridge in an airtight container for several weeks, maybe even months.

When you're ready to eat them, heat a wide-based pan with the oil until it reaches 200°C/400°F.

Fry the sticks in batches of 2 or 3; they puff in seconds so be ready to pull them out as soon as you've put them in. Use a perforated scoop to remove them, drain on kitchen paper and serve them with yuzu kosho mayo.

TEA-SMOKED PORK SCRATCHINGS

I guess these aren't proper 'scratchings', as they are a fair bit lighter. Maybe it's best to describe them as porky prawn crackers. I wanted to smoke these and to get the smoke to impregnate the skins enough to remain after frying, but to do so we had to create a dangerous amount of smoke. It used to scare the shit out of front of house staff who didn't know what we were up to. Thankfully, no harm was done! Anyway, the alternative is to give them a quick blast of smoking before serving.

SERVES 2 AS PART OF A MULTI-COURSE MENU

200g pork belly skin
700ml dashi (see page 245)
4cm piece kombu
1 litre rapeseed oil, for deep-frying
smoke mix (see page 104)

Simmer the pork belly skin with the dashi, 400ml of water and the kombu, for about 1½ hours, or until very soft. You should be able to easily poke your finger through the skin when it's done.

Remove the skin from the liquid and allow to drain and cool. Scrape away the majority of the fat from the skin and throw it away once done. (You could leave it on if you like, but the scratchings won't be as crunchy and you'll have to lower your oil temperature when frying to around 170°C/340°F.)

Cut the skin into roughly 5cm pieces and dehydrate on full heat for 6 hours or until as hard as plastic. No dehydrator? Put the skin in the oven on its lowest setting (or around 110°C/90°C fan/Gas Mark ¼) – it might take a little longer than 6 hours.

At this stage, you could store them in an airtight container until required.

When you need a scratching, heat clean rapeseed oil in a fryer or large pan to 200°C/400°F. Fry the skin, piece by piece. They will puff up quite quickly, and expand by about 50 per cent so take care.

Just before serving, crank up the wok and smoke for 2 minutes as per the recipe on page 104 and then serve.

COLD, RAW AND SALAD

SALMON GRAVADLAX SASHIMI WITH DILL-TRUFFLE-MISO SAUCE

Gravadlax is, of course, Swedish by nature and a most excellent example of curing fish. I once ate a version of gravadlax in a pokey little izakaya (bar) in Tokyo. It seemed kind of unorthodox at first, but then again amazing food is still amazing food - no matter where you are in the world - and rules aren't required here.

This sauce rules by itself so if you are not a big dill fan you can leave the stuff out.

SERVES 2 AS PART OF A MULTI-COURSE MENU

1 x 300g salmon fillet, skinned
a handful of salad leaves, to serve

For the gravadlax cure
50g fine sea salt
50g caster sugar
a pinch of ground white pepper
a pinch of shichimi togarashi
zest of ½ lemon
a small bunch of dill, stalks and all, roughly chopped

For the dill-truffle-miso sauce
a bunch of dill, optional
50g frozen spinach (not shop-bought – buying fresh and freezing it at home yourself will ensure it retains its bright colour)
62ml Japanese rice vinegar
10ml den miso (see page 244)
1 long green chilli, chopped (taste it – if they're blindingly hot and you're not ready to temporarily say goodbye to your taste buds, remove the white membrane and seeds)
truffle oil, to taste (go easy as this stuff can be strong. Don't choose the imposter oil known as truffle-flavoured oil, instead, spend your dosh on quality truffle oil. You'll know it when you smell it – like the first time you got high on petrol fumes!)

Start by mixing all the ingredients for the cure well – slip on a pair of rubber gloves and give it all a proper squishing. Lay a large sheet of clingfilm out on the worktop. Spread half of the cure mix over the sheet and then lay the salmon on top. Rub the remaining cure mix over the top of the salmon, making sure to give it a good rubbing to ensure the salmon is completely covered with the cure mix.

Wrap tightly and get that thing into the fridge. Hey presto, 12 hours later you will have some pretty serious gourmet salmon. Yeah boy!

To make the sauce, just mix all the ingredients together. Simple. Refrigerate until ready to use. (NB: This sauce is also pretty awesome with barbecued lobster – go experiment.)

Remove the salmon from the fridge, wipe off the cure mix and give the fish a very light rinse under cold running water. Pat it dry with kitchen paper. You can either slice it up and eat it now or for a more intense flavour, I like to chop up a load more fresh dill and rub it all over the cured salmon, re-wrap and then chill for another 30 minutes before slicing.

When it's time for some gravadlax action, grab your sharpest blade (think Paul Hogan's weapon of choice in *Crocodile Dundee* – what a ripper), cut the salmon into 3mm slices and of course snack on the trimmings (that's how chefs get through the day). Lay the salmon slices out on a serving plate in a kind of overlapping style. Put a pile of your favourite salad leaves on the plate, and then splatter with the dill-truffle-miso sauce.

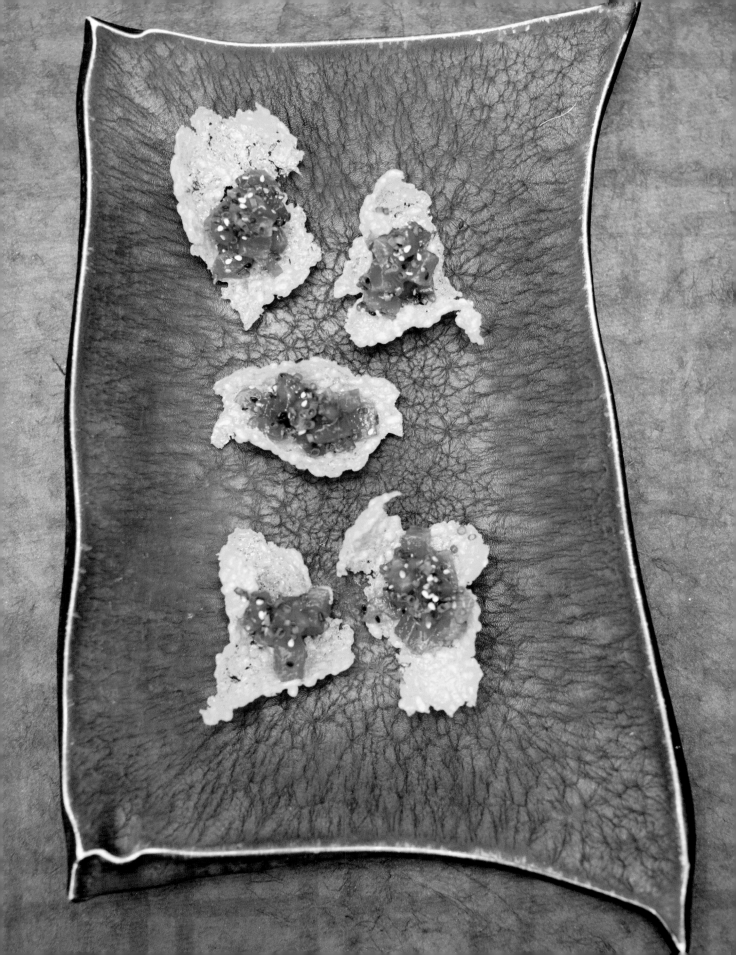

SPICY TUNA TARTARE WITH CRUNCHY SAFFRON RICE

The trouble I have with most spicy tuna dishes (maki, tartare, etc.) is that most of the time, they just ain't spicy. The name should evoke chilli heat, explosion, even Satan comes to mind. So, when I say spicy, I mean take off your skirt, cancel your manicure, grow a moustache and harden the fuck up, welcome to the real spicy tuna...

SERVES 2 AS PART OF A MULTI-COURSE MENU

140g tuna, sinew removed and diced
  (allow 60–70g per person)
20ml spicy Korean miso (see page 249)
⅓ red bird's eye chilli, finely chopped

For the crunchy saffron rice senbei
75g sushi rice
2cm piece kombu
a pinch of saffron
1 litre rapeseed oil, for deep-frying

To serve
½ spring onion, chopped
1cm piece ginger, finely grated
¼ green chilli, sliced, optional

To make the crunchy saffron rice senbei, take the sushi rice, don't wash it, just whack it into a wide-based pan with loads of cold water and the kombu. Pour in enough water to cover the rice by 5cm (more water than your instinct tells you to, go on, splash out … barely a pun, was it). This is an odd one. I can't give you an exact recipe as it's all down to really overcooking the rice until it is totally fucked, a porridge of sorts. The best I can offer is to say you need to set the pan over a medium-high heat and stir often, until the mushy madness takes shape – about 45 minutes to 1 hour. You may need to add more water as the rice cooks so that it doesn't become dry.

When the rice is very soft and is the consistency of thick porridge, remove it from the heat and stir in the saffron. Allow to cool down briefly. Dip an angled palette knife or spatula into cold water to wet it, and use this to spread the rice porridge onto a non-stick baking mat. The layer should be thin, about 1mm, and spread as evenly as possible, without any holes. Dip the palette knife into cold water in between spreads to stop it from sticking.

If you have the luxury of a dehydrator then shove it in there for a few hours. It's done when it comes out like a thin sheet of translucent plastic. If you don't have one of those babies, place the baking mat on a tray in your oven with the pilot light on, or at its lowest setting for about 12 hours. If it only dries on one side, flip 'er over and continue until totally dried. Keep the dried rice sheet in an airtight container until needed.

An hour or so before serving, heat the oil in your fryer or a large pan to 220°C/425°F. Carefully drop in 1 or 2 pieces of rice sheet at a time – they puff up extremely quickly, a bit like a prawn cracker. Once puffed, remove the senbei with a perforated scoop and drain on a wire rack before transferring to kitchen paper to drain completely. Put on a tray in a very low oven to keep warm whilst you prepare the tuna.

Now, for the spicy tuna tartare straight from Satan's pantry. Put the diced tuna in a bowl, squirt over the spicy Korean miso and throw in the chopped chilli. Mix well.

To serve, break your puffed saffron senbei into large bite-sized pieces and top with some spicy tuna tartare, chopped spring onion, grated fresh ginger and a couple of slices of green chilli. PACK SOME HEAT.

YELLOWTAIL SASHIMI WITH KIZAMI WASABI SALSA AND YUZU SOY

Yellowtail might refer to several different species of fish - it depends who's telling the story, I suppose. In this case, I am on about the Japanese fish hamachi (amberjack). I could carry on forever about how amazing it is and how wonderful the texture is but that won't do. You need to eat it. Do a search, the Japanese send it all over the world and it is worth seeking out. Alternatively, use salmon if the yellowtail thang ain't happening for you.

SERVES 2 AS PART OF A MULTI-COURSE MENU

120–130g yellowtail (hamachi) fish (ideally, ask your supplier to give you a head-end section from the fillet; it should be a section about 10cm x 4–5cm)

For the kizami wasabi salsa
½ small white onion, finely diced
75g pickled wasabi stem (kizami wasabi)
25ml grapeseed oil
¼ long cucumber, seeds removed and finely diced
juice of ¼ lime
4 shiso or mint leaves, finely chopped
a pinch of sea salt

For the yuzu soy
50ml yuzu juice
125ml dark soy sauce
juice of ¼ lime

To serve
¼–1 green chilli, sliced
shredded daikon, optional
shredded cucumber, optional
shredded carrot, optional

First, make the salsa. Simply mix the ingredients, seal in a container and refrigerate for up to 4–5 days.

To make the yuzu soy, mix the ingredients and store in the refrigerator. This is really useful to have ready for loads of other dishes (finishing sauce for a stir fry, crispy oysters or tofu salad dressing, for example), so feel free to double up the quantities and keep in the fridge for later use.

When you're ready to serve, prepare the sashimi. Hold the fillet on a 25 degree angle to your cutting board and then cut the slices with your knife held at (about) an 85 degree angle. You should aim for about ½cm-thick slices – a little thinner if you can.

Roll up your yellowtail slices and arrange in a bit of a semi-circle on your best sashimi serving plate. Put a small dollop of the salsa on each sashimi slice and add a snippet of green chilli to top it off. Drizzle with some of the yuzu soy mixture, or put some in a small dipping cup to have on the side.

At the restaurants we mix together shredded daikon, cucumber and carrot and pile a mound of this as a garnish – it freshens those taste buds after you've had your way with the yellowtail.

HIJIKI SALAD

Hijiki is a kind of seaweed, which you can find dried in Japanese food stores and online. Going back a few years there was a concern that hijiki was somehow dangerous for our health that led to a temporary ban in the UK. Turns out somebody couldn't quite prove their point, so back it came. In Japan, they believe that this stuff makes for good, strong, healthy hair... Balding blokes listen up!

This can be a killer side dish or a very satisfying light - and not forgetting hair-boosting - meal by adding a few optional extras.

SERVES 2 AS PART OF A MULTI-COURSE MENU

For the hijiki

100g hijiki, soaked in cold water for 3
   hours and drained well
250ml dashi (see page 245)
110ml dark soy sauce
60g caster sugar
100ml
5ml mirin
20ml sesame oil

To serve (optional extras, choose any of the following)

shredded carrot
freshly podded peas
edamame beans
ripe avocado, destoned and cut
   into chunks
flaked cooked salmon
diced tofu
grilled chicken
cooked grains, especially that trendy
   bugger quinoa
Japanese sesame seeds

Combine all the ingredients for the hijiki in a large pan over a medium heat and bring to a simmer. Cover and cook for about 45 minutes. Test for doneness by eating a few pieces of hijiki – it should be fairly tender. Remove from the heat and cool to room temperature, leaving it in the pan with all of the cooking juices. Decant into a bowl or container if you wish, cover and refrigerate. Once cooked, the hijiki keeps for up to 2–3 weeks so this can be done well in advance.

Once chilled, you can serve it as is, or with any of the optional extras as a side dish. For example, place the shredded carrot, fresh peas or edamame beans in a small bowl, sprinkle with sesame seeds and add a few tablespoons of the hijiki juices as a dressing.

SALMON TATAKI WITH SWEET POTATO CRISPS AND WASABI MAYO

This involves a cool technique that gives the salmon a killer barbecue-like flavour on the exterior whilst leaving the interior raw; you actually get the best of both worlds - barbecue tastiness with the wondrous texture and taste of sashimi. Even if you don't like salmon sashimi still give this a bash. It may well be the thing that sways you as it's a pretty good compromise. Tofu, beef and scallops also work well in place of the salmon.

SERVES 2 AS PART OF A MULTI-COURSE MENU

1 x 100g salmon fillet
red chilli, sliced, to serve, optional
sea salt and freshly ground black pepper,
    to taste

For the wasabi mayo
100g mayonnaise
15g good-quality wasabi paste
8g lemon juice
a pinch of sea salt

For the sweet potato crisps
1 small–medium orange sweet potato
1 litre rapeseed oil, for deep-frying

To serve
wasabi tobiko
wedge of lime

Quickly prepare the wasabi mayo by mixing all the ingredients together and leave in the fridge until needed.

Tataki is all about searing the piece of meat or fish as fast and hot as you can before the heat starts to cook the internal flesh. To do this, heat a pan until scorching hot over a high heat. Season the salmon with salt and pepper and get it into the hot pan. Sear the salmon for about 10 seconds on each side, or until coloured (you want the salmon to brown as quickly as possible before the heat cooks it through). Immediately remove from the pan and leave to cool to room temperature. Some people like to plunge it into iced water to stop the cooking properly, but I think this just washes away the flavour of the fish. Slice the seared salmon on an angle into 2–3mm-thick pieces.

While the salmon comes to room temperature, prepare the sweet potato crisps. Peel the sweet potato and then, holding the potato in one hand and a peeler in the other, rotate the potato, one turn at a time, to get peel-like strips of the sweet potato which look a bit like orange peelings, without any skin.

Heat the oil in your fryer or a large pan to 180°C/350°F. Fry the sweet potato strips in small batches until they are golden. Drain on kitchen paper and keep in a warm place.

To serve, arrange the tataki slices randomly around the plate, prop some up with sweet potato crisps, then scatter the remaining sweet potato around. Do some wild drizzling of the wasabi mayo around your plate and top with some slices of red chilli if you like. Hit it with a scattering of wasabi tobiko to really re-inforce your wasabi intention. A wedge of lime on the side is a nice touch too. Serve up!

SOBA PANCAKES WITH KING CRAB AND YUZU KOSHO

When I was a kid my mum used to make these tiny flat pancakes, known in Australia as pikelets. We used to eat them once they had cooled down with butter and sometimes other sprinkles or toppings. I suppose I was kind of thinking about pikelets when I thought of this. The initial idea I had was for a crab omelette and somehow I ended up with more of a crab pancake... Anyway, the result is a little pancake-pikelet, used to scoop up some creamy crab. The pikelet can scoop up other bits and pieces too. It doesn't take a smart-ass restaurant critic-brainiac to figure out that mashed-up avocado or a baby prawn cocktail would also become rather capable partners.

SERVES 6-8

For the crab

200g cooked king crabmeat (use any other good-quality crabmeat as a substitute. Posh cat food in a can doesn't count!)

60g Japanese Kewpie mayonnaise

20g yuzu kosho paste (no substitutes! Buy it online if you're a proper self-proclaimed 'foodie')

a splash of lemon juice

a splash of dark soy sauce

2 tablespoons chopped red onion

2 tablespoons chopped chives, plus extra to serve

¼ nori sheet, crushed, to serve

sea salt and freshly ground black pepper

For the soba pancakes

220g plain flour

120g soba (buckwheat) flour

5g sea salt

2 eggs plus 1 egg yolk, lightly beaten

120g nut-brown butter (see note below)

650ml full-cream milk

60g cooked soba grains (or use buckwheat grains if you can't source soba)

grapeseed or light olive oil, for frying

First, make the creamy crab mixture. Pick through the crabmeat to make sure it's free from any stray shells. Mix with all the other ingredients, then you're good to go. Taste for seasoning. You could do this in advance, like the night before, but I wouldn't do it any further in advance than that.

To make the pancakes, combine the flours and sea salt, and mix well. Form a well in the middle of the flour mix. Pour in the lightly beaten eggs, nut-brown butter and the milk.

Whisk, starting with the stuff in the centre of the little well. Mix vigorously, slowly incorporating the flour from the edges. Once combined, whisk like mad until the batter is mega-smooth.

Whack it in the fridge to chill out for at least 1 hour before cooking. Once the mixture is nicely rested, heat a non-stick pan until moderately hot. WTF does that mean? Hot but not scorching.

Add some oil to the pan. Using a large teaspoon, drop in enough batter to form 6–7cm-diameter pancakes. Sprinkle each one with some of the cooked soba grains.

Allow the pancakes to cook on the first side until little air bubbles start to form on the raw side, flip 'em over and cook for a further minute. Keep going until you have enough for your little crab feast.

To serve it up you have two options:

Slack asses – At the very least, put all the crab mixture into a pretty bowl and top with some extra chives. Serve with a teaspoon and the soba pancakes on the side. Your guests may feel mildly disappointed at your laziness, but you should win them back once they taste it.

Fancy asses – Carefully put a big teaspoon of the crab mixture in the centre of a pancake and fold up the sides to form a kind of taco. Put a skewer through to hold it together. (I use a split skewer called a matsuba gushi; it's like a little double skewer held together at one end.) Do the chive sprinkle, top with some crumbled or crushed nori sheet and then knock 'em dead with your artful coolness.

Note: To make nut-brown butter take a lump of good-quality salted butter, whack it in a saucepan and cook it over a medium-high heat until it starts to bubble, change colour and smell nutty, probably after around 8–10 minutes. Remove from the heat quickly, strain through a muslin-lined sieve into a bowl. Discard the solids.

ICED SWEET AND SOUR NASU

This is a summertime cracker. Nasu is the Japanese word for aubergine and the long thin purple ones are one of the varieties specific to Japan. For this recipe, I use the common, everyday big dark purple aubergine.

Baking aubergine in den miso sauce (see page 244) has converted so many customers at Kurobuta (who normally hate the stuff). Cooking it this way highlights what an amazing texture aubergine can have, as does this recipe. It winds up being almost jelly-like and slippery sounds odd? It is, but also very refreshing served over ice. A welcomed curve ball served amongst some other dishes.

The technique and liquor comes from a traditional method of preparation, used mainly for fish, called nanban zuke (see page 247), which was introduced as escabeche by the Portuguese many moons ago.

SERVES 2 AS PART OF A MULTI-COURSE MENU

1 large purple aubergine
potato starch, for dusting
1 litre rapeseed oil, for deep-frying
nanban zuke base (see page 247)

To serve
1 large fresh red chilli, thinly sliced
a small pinch of white sesame seeds
coriander leaves, optional
crushed ice

Peel the aubergine and cut it into approximately 3cm cubes. They don't need to be perfect – rough is OK. Toss the aubergine cubes in the potato starch to coat.

Heat up the oil in your fryer or a large pan to 180°C/350°F. When hot enough, carefully drop the aubergine into the hot oil and deep-fry for 2½–3 minutes, until golden and cooked right the way through. Do this in batches if necessary. Remove to drain on a wire rack before transferring to kitchen paper to drain completely. Place in a bowl and generously cover the fried aubergine pieces with the nanban zuke mix. Allow to cool to room temperature and then refrigerate for a good 12 hours.

To serve, gently transfer the aubergine cubes to a serving bowl, pour over some of the nanban zuke juices, enough to leave a decent-sized puddle on the bottom of the bowl. Top with some chilli and sesame seeds and, whilst we are breaking rules, add some picked coriander too if you wish. Serve over a big bowl of crushed ice.

RAZOR CLAM SALAD WITH GRAPEFRUIT AND TOSAZU

These little buggers can be a bit tricky to remove from their shells - they are called razor clams with good reason. If you mess around too much with razor clams, you'll have some chewy shit to deal with. In this recipe I blanch them in boiling dashi, and super-quickly at that. Another good thing to do is toss them in some butter, garlic and soy in a scorching hot pan for a few seconds. Get them out fast though, as they will carry on cooking a little with the residual heat.

SERVES 2 AS PART OF A MULTI-COURSE MENU

4 fresh razor clams
750ml dashi (see page 245)

For the tosazu
65ml dark soy sauce
35ml Japanese black vinegar
65ml Japanese rice vinegar
5g katsuobushi (bonito flakes)

To serve
½ pink grapefruit, peeled and segmented
2 rashers streaky bacon, fried until crisp and broken into crumbs or small pieces

First, make the tosazu. Combine all the ingredients for the tosazu in a stainless steel bowl or container and cover with clingfilm. Leave to 'mature' for 2 days at room temperature. Then strain through a sieve lined with muslin into a clean container and refrigerate until the end of time.

Next, prepare the clams. Use a regular table knife to carefully prize open the shell; it will open on one side and be hinged on the other. With the same knife, gently scrape the flesh away from the shell and put it into a bowl. Keep the shells and ensure they are free of all meat. Bring a pan of water to the boil and drop the shells in, boiling them for 4–5 minutes to kill off any raw juices or nasties. Drain and rinse the shells well in cold water, and set aside to use for presentation.

Now use a sharp knife to detach the thicker, fleshier part of the clam from the thinner, stingier part, and remove the black part too. Make an incision down the length of each of the thicker parts, just enough so they can lie flat. Rinse them under cold running water and rinse the thinner parts very well as sand often gets lodged in the hard-to-get-to parts.

Bring the dashi to the boil and have a large bowl of iced water ready (the clams will be plunged into the water to stop them from cooking once blanched).

Cook the thicker clams in a couple of batches by putting them into a perforated scoop (aka spider) and lowering into the hot dashi. Give them a quick shake, about 2 or 3 seconds, then remove and plunge into the bowl of iced water. Repeat with the thinner clams, which will require a very quick dip. Blanch them in small batches to ensure they are cooked as evenly as possible.

To serve, divide the clams between their shells, top with the grapefruit and bacon pieces and then drizzle over the tosazu.

CHILLED SOMEN NOODLES IN SHIITAKE DIPPING BROTH

I might even argue that these noodles are equally as refreshing as an ice-cold beer on a hot summer's day. Somen are thin wheat-based noodles and excellent for slurping. One of the keys to making this dish shit-hot is the little extras, or 'garnishes' if you like. You can add other stuff to make it more interesting too - fresh umi (sea urchin) for instance is pretty awesome. When it comes to wasabi, I'm not talking about that bright green rubbish in the little tubes because you're better off with a high-quality wasabi powder. Better still, use the fresh stuff - it's out there.

SERVES 2

120g dried somen (noodles)

50g kimchi pickle (see page 246)

3 spring onions, thinly sliced then washed and drained well

6g wasabi powder, mixed with enough water to make a thick paste

15g ginger, grated

500ml chilled shiitake broth (see below)

For the shiitake broth

120g dried shiitake mushrooms

450ml water

80ml dark soy sauce

80ml mirin

80ml sake

2–3cm piece kombu

For the shiitake tetsuzuke

50g dried shiitake mushrooms, soaked in cold water for 2 hours

30ml mirin

80ml dark soy sauce

80g caster sugar

100ml sake

For the tempura crunchies

500ml rapeseed oil, for deep-frying

20ml trisol batter (see page 251)

To serve

crushed ice

bamboo leaves

To make the basis of the broth, soak the dried shiitake in the water overnight, then strain the liquid into a clean bowl. (The rehydrated shiitake can be used in a hotpot, stir-fry or to make the shiitake tetsuzuke – see below.)

Mix the shiitake water with the remaining ingredients for the broth and allow the kombu to steep for 2 hours. Strain off and you're good to go. Serve hot or cold. This can be made in advance and stored in the fridge where it will keep for up to 2 weeks.

To make the shiitake tetsuzuke, combine all the ingredients in a pan and bring to the boil. Boil for 30 seconds and then allow to cool. Chill for at least 1 hour before use, or store until needed (it will keep longer than you and I).

Next make the tempura crunchies. Heat the oil in a fryer or large pan to 180°C/350°F. Once heated, allow lots of small droplets of tempura batter to fall in. Fry for 45 seconds until golden. Remove with a perforated scoop, drain well on kitchen paper and set aside in a warm place until ready to use.

Next, cook your somen noodles in rapidly boiling water – make sure there is excess water as you want the noodles to have room to move around and absorb the water. Using a small pan that is only half full will result in a big clump of doughy crap. Remember – big pot boiling! The noodles will take around 2 minutes to be fully cooked. Drain, rinse well under cold running water and then set aside.

Now it's a matter of gathering your garnishes and making sure that your shiitake broth is chilled.

The best way to present this dish is on a bed of crushed ice. Ice cubes won't work, but if that's all you have then throw them into a plastic bag and beat the shit out of them with a rolling pin – ta-da, bashed ice! So, ice on the bottom of a deep-ish platter, then top the ice with a few bamboo leaves so that your ingredients aren't going directly onto the ice.

Arrange a nice pile of noodles to one side, then make little piles of the kimchi, tempura crunchies, spring onions, wasabi, grated ginger and some sliced shiitake tetsuzuke.

You should serve about 200–250ml of shiitake the broth per person. Pour 100ml or so of the chilled broth into each serving bowl, the rest can be put in a communal jug on the side. At the table, simply help yourselves to some noodles and some of the garnishes, a little at a time. Munch, sip (right outta the soup bowl) then repeat. The broth will gain depth of flavour from the garnishes being added to it so adding fresh broth is essential, plus it's tasty as hell – you'll want to keep on sipping away at it.

SALMON AND FOIE GRAS KOBU-JIME IN FUJI APPLE AND OYSTER CREAM

Kobu-jime is a classic preparation, whereby (usually) fish is wrapped in kombu to marinate for a period. The idea is that the kombu imparts a shit-ton of umami into the fish, as well as firming it up slightly.

I used to mess about with foie gras when I first came to London - I hadn't really been in an environment that would allow Japanese-inspired techniques with such things as foie gras. I tried loads of stuff and inflicted each experiment on the lucky (and possibly sometimes unlucky) customers of Nobu in Park Lane. This was perhaps my favourite technique out of the sixty-plus experiments that took place. The foie gras is kind of cured and winds up being mega creamy - there is no need to cook it further, just slice and serve.

SERVES 2 OR 3 AS PART OF A MULTI-COURSE MENU

25cm piece kombu, broken into 2 pieces
sake, for soaking
90g foie gras
½ green chilli, sliced
a small handful of katsuobushi (bonito flakes)
2–3 tablespoons sea salt

For the oyster cream

75ml double cream
2 star anise
5 fresh rock oysters, shucked and drained
50ml dashi (see page 245)
½ tablespoon light soy sauce
a pinch of sea salt

To finish

3 slices salmon sashimi
10cm x 10cm sheet crunchy rice senbei (see page 33, but omit the saffron)
½ Fuji apple, skin on, finely diced
20ml spicy shiso ponzu (see page 249)
fresh or frozen yuzu zest
a few green chilli slices
chives, finely chopped

Soak the kombu in a small bowl of sake for 2 minutes. Drain.

Cut the foie gras into 30g slices, approximately 1cm thick. Place on top of one of the kombu pieces and sprinkle with the sea salt. Scatter over the green chilli slices then dump the katsuobushi over the top. Place the other piece of kombu on top, then wrap the little foie gras/kombu sandwich tightly with clingfilm. Refrigerate for at least 5–6 hours before use.

To make the oyster cream, bring the cream and star anise to a gentle boil in a saucepan. Simmer for about 5 minutes to infuse the cream and allow to reduce by about half. Take off the heat and cool. Strain the cream into a jug and throw away the star anise. Just before serving, blend all the remaining ingredients for the oyster cream with the reduced cream in a blender or using a stick blender. Give the cream another strain, then blend again to get a smooth cream.

Remove the foie gras from the kombu, leaving the katsuobushi and chilli intact if possible. Cut the foie gras into 5mm-thick strips.

Arrange the foie gras strips and the salmon sashimi on the senbei rice crackers. Toss the Fuji apple in the ponzu sauce, and add a few chunks to each senbei.

Spoon over the oyster cream, then top with the yuzu zest, some green chilli slices and chives. Eat, quickly!

JUNK FOOD JAPAN

TUNA SASHIMI PIZZA

I have my friend Ahmed Almoayed to thank for this one. Ahmed has a happening Japanese joint in Bahrain called Mirai, in fact I used to work for him, and often still do some consultancy out there for him. He once mentioned that he had heard about somebody doing this in the States and wanted me to develop it for Mirai. I thought, this can't be good – how on earth can I make this taste good,

it's such cheesy Americanised junk. So I messed about with it and left him with a version. As we were opening the Kurobuta pop-up in Chelsea, I remembered the pizza and Junk Food Japan was born! How do I feel about it now? It's a guilty pleasure, and I love it! If you're not keen on tuna, do the exact same recipe with slices of avocado, or try it with salmon if tuna ain't your thang!

SERVES 2 AS PART OF A MULTI-COURSE MENU (1 PIZZA IS GOOD FOR 2 AS A FATTY SNACK OR AS PART OF A KUROBUTA FEAST)

1 soft tortilla wrap (not the big thick one; the thinner the better)

1 litre rapeseed oil, for deep-frying

64g fresh tuna, or 8 sashimi slices (you should have two 8–10g sashimi slices per pizza 'quarter')

¼ red onion, finely diced

½ green chilli, finely diced

2 teaspoons wasabi tobiko (fish roe)

black and white sesame seeds, for sprinkling

chopped chives, optional

For the truffle ponzu

100g Japanese Kewpie mayonnaise

20ml ponzu sauce (see page 247)

a few drops of white truffle oil

To make the truffle ponzu, whisk the mayonnaise and ponzu sauce together, season with the truffle oil, and you are ready to rock. Any leftover sauce can be used for salads or tempura or as a dip for raw veg/crudités.

To make a pizza base (of sorts), find a bowl that is around 15cm in diameter and tip it over onto the tortilla, then run a knife around the bowl so that you end up with a 15cm pizza base.

Crank the fryer up to 180°C/350°F. Don't use the crusty old oil that you left in the pan from the last time you got high and decided to make your own KFC! In your pristine oil, fry the pizza base for between 2 and 3 minutes until crunchy – it will come out looking like it's had a good old session on a sun bed.

Use metal tongs to remove the base from the oil, drain on kitchen paper and allow to cool briefly. When you think you can take the heat (don't let it cool down too much as it will break easily), take a bread knife and cut the base evenly into quarters. Place on some kitchen paper and leave in a fairly warm place to drain any excess oil.

To slice the tuna – what a boring explanation that would be, 'using your right hand as an extension to your soul… blah … blah'. Check the photos, they speak to you.

Right, let's pizza. Find a sexy plate and arrange your crunchy pizza base in the shape of a, wait for it … pizza! Shock! Give your base a light drizzle with the truffle ponzu, then proceed to drape the tuna slices over so that you cover most of the surface of the base. Top with a scattering of diced onion, chillies, wasabi tobiko and finally the sesame seeds.

Just before you drip this all over your new snakeskin boots, give it another drizzle of the truffle ponzu. One last tip, if you have a sharp knife and you dig chives, finely chop some, and tip all over the pizza.

If the day ever comes I'd like to be buried in a giant pizza box, from Japan of course. Rest in pizza…

BARBECUED PORK RIBS WITH STICKY HONEY, SOY AND GINGER GLAZE

No barbecue is complete without ribs. I don't mean lightweight champions, the lamb ribs, or those caveman-like beef ribs, nor do I mean short ribs or pigeon ribs for that matter. I'm talking PORK! The word rib should be reclassed from a cookery standpoint so it only refers to pork in my view.

This is another great example of how doing some simple prep work the day before your barbecue will pay off.

Rib meat is pretty tough and so to get the best out of them you'll need to slow cook them and let them cool down in their cooking juices. When it comes to barbecuing, you'll need to grill them up, cold beer in one hand, tongs in the other, reciting dad jokes to your guests: so cool!

SERVES 4 AS PART OF A MULTI-COURSE FEAST, OR 2 GREEDY BUGGERS

1kg pork ribs, cut into 7–8 racks
2 tablespoons grapeseed oil, for grilling the ribs

For the master stock
1 whole garlic bulb, cut in half horizontally
6 spring onions
1 large knob of ginger (about 6cm), cut into 3 or 4 chunks
1 long red chilli, cut in half
10cm piece kombu
1 brown onion, cut in half
500ml dark soy sauce

For the soy-mirin glaze
50ml dark soy sauce
50ml mirin

For the honey, soy and ginger glaze
160g liquid honey
35g grated ginger
1 tablespoon dark soy sauce
25g fresh lemon juice

To serve
black and/or white sesame seeds
½ red onion, finely sliced
½ green chilli, finely sliced

To make the stock, put all the ingredients in a large pan with 5 litresof water. Bring to the boil and simmer for 2 hours, skimming off any scum that comes to the surface. Remove from the heat and allow to cool to room temperature.

Rinse the pork ribs and pat dry with kitchen paper. Place the ribs into your room temperature master stock and bring up to a light simmer. Allow to simmer over a medium-high heat for around 1½ hours. The timing will depend on the pork itself, so this is a rough guide; the meat needs to fall away from the bone easily. When done, remove the pan from the heat and allow the ribs to cool to room temperature in the master stock.

Use a slotted spoon to remove the ribs from the stock and transfer to a container or bowl. Cover and refrigerate for 2 hours.

Strain the stock into a large container and chill in the fridge until required. You can keep this base stock for ages (seriously, provided that it is boiled before each use, cooled properly before being refrigerated, you can keep the stock going for months or even years). It also freezes well if you're a little suspect.

To make the soy-mirin glaze, combine the two ingredients in a spray bottle. To make the honey, soy and ginger glaze, mix all the ingredients well. Set both glazes aside.

Light your barbecue and get it hot.

Lightly oil the ribs and whack 'em on the barbie. We like to barbecue ours over charcoal but you could do them just as well on a solid, cast-iron surface.

Barbecue the ribs until they take on a little colour, spraying with the mirin-soy glaze every 30–40 seconds to allow the ribs to glaze up and get nice and sticky. When shiny hot and smelling fine, remove from the barbecue.

Get that pork on your fork... Drench the cooked ribs in the honey, soy and ginger glaze. Scatter with some sesame seeds and the red onion and green chilli. Now get dirty!

MISO GRILLED HOT WINGS

I don't know many people who can say no to a good wing. As with other slightly tougher cuts of meat, I like to slow cook the wings first before giving them some barbecue action. I give the wings a drizzle with some spicy miso sauce while they're grilling, but you could easily change it up and drizzle them with some sriracha, spray them in mirin and soy, or just keep them plain, served with sea salt and lemon.

SERVES 2 AS PART OF A MULTI-COURSE MENU

20 chicken wings
3 litres master stock (see page 63),
   at room temperature
2 tablespoons grapeseed oil, for cooking

For the spicy miso sauce
160g gochujang (fermented chilli paste)
50g Japanese rice vinegar
15ml sake
35g sugar
50ml dashi (see page 245)
25g white miso paste
1 egg yolk

To serve (optional)
lemon wedges
sesame seeds
spring onions

Prepare the chicken wings by removing the tip and disconnecting the centre from the part that looks like a mini drumstick.

Rinse and pat the wings dry with kitchen paper, then place in a large pan with the room temperature stock. Bring up to a simmer and cook for 1½ hours, until the meat becomes soft.

Take off the heat and let the stock cool down to room temperature. Remove the chicken from the stock, cover in clingfilm and refrigerate for at least 1 hour to firm up.

Make up the spicy miso sauce. Mix all the ingredients except the egg yolk in a blender. Put the mix in a saucepan and cook over a very low heat for 15 minutes – do not boil. Cool to room temperature, then whisk in the egg yolk. Chill and keep forever (or until you're ready to serve).

Time to crank up the barbecue.

Toss the wings in a little oil then get them onto your very hot barbecue. There isn't a great alternative if you have no barbecue, but if that is the case, then you could use a salamander grill, or, though I haven't tried this yet, a sandwich press might work.

Get a nice barbecue-scorched colour on the wings and, at that point, drizzle some of the spicy miso sauce over them. Jostle the wings around until the miso starts to caramelise. Get 'em off…

Toss over a little more sauce, then serve up immediately.

Get fancy by squeezing some fresh lemon over the top before eating, and maybe some sesame seeds, too. Go crazy and serve with some lightly grilled spring onions.

CRUNCHY CHICKEN KARA-AGE BUNS WITH SPICY MAYO AND CUCUMBER PICKLE

Ok, this is some proper junk food - fried chicken in a bun. Still think Japanese food is all about purity? Get to know Japan, even just a little, and you will soon realise that they like to fry chicken just like the rest of us. I'd be surprised to find an izakaya that didn't feature chicken kara-age. It's a classic. Dare I mention the Colonel? They embrace his secret recipe chicken, so much so that they now serve beer at KFCs in Japan, so you can soak up your fried goodness with a cool ambery swallow.

MAKES 12 BUNS

3 chicken thighs, skinless and boneless,
potato starch, for coating
1 litre rapeseed oil, for deep-frying

For the chicken kara-mara marinade

1 tablespoon curry power
1 tablespoon cornflour
1 tablespoon plain flour
1½ teaspoons fine salt
1 teaspoon finely ground black pepper
1 teaspoon caster sugar
1 tablespoon Shaoxing wine
1 tablespoon garlic purée
1 tablespoon ginger purée

For the buns

325g bread flour
15g milk powder
2g baking powder
½ teaspoon fine sea salt
30g caster sugar
20g fresh yeast
190ml lukewarm water
35g lard, melted until liquid, or light
   olive oil

For the spicy mayo

200g Japanese Kewpie mayonnaise
80g sriracha sauce
juice of 1 lime

To serve

iceberg lettuce
green chillies, sliced
quick cucumber pickles (see page 248),
   optional

First make the chicken kara-mara marinade by mixing all the ingredients together. Cut each chicken thigh into 4 and rub well with the marinade. Leave for 24 hours, or at the very least, give it a couple of hours.

To make the buns, mix 50ml of warm water with the yeast. Allow the yeast to soften for 3–4 minutes, then whisk in another 140ml of warm water.

Meanwhile, combine the flour, milk powder, baking powder, salt and sugar in the bowl of an electric mixer and use clean dry hands to mix well. With the dough hook attached, set the mixer on a medium speed. Slowly pour the yeast and warm water mixture into the dry mix and mix to combine fully. Ramp up the speed a little and slowly pour in the lard (or light olive oil, which will still give you a pretty good result).

If the mix looks a little too wet – like, if you pick it up and it's just pure goo – then mix in a little more flour; if it's too dry then drizzle in some more water. Once it's looking as it should, slow the mixer back down to a medium speed and let it keep on mixing for 20 minutes.

Lightly grease a stainless steel bowl and tip your well-worked dough in, cover with clingfilm and sit the bowl in a nice warm place to double in size, AKA – grow or rise. Once your dough has doubled, knock it back, or, to put it simply, give it a punch and knock the air out of it. Work it back into a ball, then stretch it out into a long, snake-like shape (more python than green tree snake).

Now, you need to divide the snake up into 30g chunks; use a knife that is crappy and not really loved anymore. Work fast, or the dough will start to rise yet again and we don't want that just yet.

Next, we are going to roll these chunks into balls. Press the palm of your hand down, firmly, onto one of the chunks, and move it around anticlockwise allowing it to form a ball as you work it. Put the balls onto a deep tray lined with baking parchment.

Once you have finished rolling, you can either freeze your balls until you need them or carry on with the final stages of the process. If you have chosen to freeze them and want to carry on, then simply defrost and crack on with the next instruction. (This recipe makes 20 buns, so you can freeze 8 to use later anyway.)

recipe continued on page 72

Position the buns in a warm place, lightly covered with clingfilm, making sure the film isn't touching the buns (putting them in a lipped, deep tray is best). Once the buns have doubled in size and look light and fluffy, they are ready to be steamed once you've assembled all the other components.

Make the mayo by mixing the ingredients together well. Set aside.

Heat the oil in your fryer to 180°C/350°F. Wipe the majority of the marinade from the chicken then coat well in the potato starch. Rub it in really well, adding more potato starch as required. When you think you've given it enough, massage it again; there will be a few damp spots and we want to make sure each and every part of the chicken is rubbed with plenty of starch.

Carefully drop the chicken pieces into the hot oil and deep-fry for 4–5 minutes – the thickness of your chicken thighs will determine if it's more or less. Remove and drain well on a perforated tray or wire rack placed over a baking tray. Fry in batches if necessary.

While the chicken is draining, steam the buns for 10 minutes.

Lets bun…

I always torch the exterior of my buns with a blowtorch (little wonder there's no hair left on 'em!). This makes them taste toasty and firms them up a little bit – optional but preferable.

Cut your buns through the middle, add a big squirt of the spicy mayo, some iceberg lettuce and sliced green chillies, top with a crunchy chunk of chicken kara-age, then give another squirt of the spicy mayo. Top it off with some more chillies if you're hungover and need your ass kicked for being so stoopid! I serve pickled cucumbers on the side as they make a good palate cleanser (and I have a pickle fetish). Shove them in the bun, whatever you fancy, they just fit well.

FRIED CHICKEN PARTY

'You can't compare apples with apples', where did that saying come from? Well, it doesn't matter too much, I'm hijacking it. 'You can't compare fried chicken with fried chicken.' It's like anything I suppose, you get the good and the bad. Fried chicken often cops the bad press, and we probably all think of that silver-haired old fox, the Colonel. You may also think Americana, and why not - where else would you find such a geezer? But this geezer is a global dude and Japan is no exception. In Japan, you can even pre-order your KFC Christmas feast.

Frying chicken isn't all about Southern-style seasoning and shitty coleslaw on the side. In Japan, plump chunks of marinated chicken are dusted in katakuriko (a kind of potato starch) then fried up and served with a wedge of lemon, some salt or a basic ponzu-type dip - the ultimate beer-drinking snack by the way.

I don't see why we shouldn't serve fried chicken in the restaurants; it's another of those lovely guilty pleasures and you can bet your ass it sells! This is food that shouldn't be taken too seriously: yes you need to use the best quality free-range, corn-fed and well-reared chicken as possible, but you shouldn't think this sort of food is beneath your fancy repertoire of recipes you can't even pronounce properly. Yes, it's a 'sometimes food' and when executed properly it will bring on a devilish cheeky grin that ought to be reserved for other naughtiness.

Throw a fried chicken party and watch the cheeky grins appear from the corner of your friends' mouths. Party on chicken lovers!

SERVES A PARTY FOR 2

1 whole baby chicken, or poussin (fancy
   French name, pronounced poo-san,
   which would be very rude in Japanese)
2 litres master stock (see page 63)
1 egg yolk
100ml single cream
100ml full-cream milk
2 litres rapeseed oil, for deep-frying

For the crunchy fry flour

150g tempura flour
2 tablespoons dried oregano
1 tablespoon dried thyme
1½ tablespoons cayenne pepper
1½ tablespoons shichimi, plus extra
   to serve
2 tablespoons ground black pepper
¼ tablespoon potato starch

To serve

flaked sea salt
big dollop of kimchi mayonnaise (see
   page 246)
spicy shiso ponzu (see page 249)
red and green chillies, chopped, optional
lemon wedges
ice-cold sake, some wet shots and some
   frosty beer

Cut the chicken into 10 pieces: each breast into 2, remove the wings (hopefully you have 2 of these), remove and then separate the drumsticks and thigh meat.

Heat the master stock to 85°C/185°F in a large pan and plonk your chicken pieces in. Maintain the temperature and cook for 25 minutes. Take off the heat and cool the chicken in the stock to room temperature, and then remove the chicken and refrigerate, covered in clingfilm. You can store the master stock in the fridge or freeze for future use – just boil it before each use. The stock will keep for weeks and will get stronger every time it is boiled, just top it up with some water on each occasion and skim any scum off the surface.

Whip up the egg yolk and mix with it the cream and milk. Soak the chicken in this mix for 20 minutes.

To make the crunchy fry flour, mix all the ingredients well and store in a cool, dry place.

Now for the frying. Heat up the rapeseed oil in a large pan until it hits 180°C/350°F. Maintain this temperature.

Take the soaked chicken pieces and dip them into the crunchy fry flour – give them a really thorough rub, then toss about so that all the chicken pieces are well coated and there are no wet spots left.

Fry the chicken pieces immediately. Check the temperature of your oil once the chicken goes in. If the temperature rapidly reduces, give it some more heat so that it gets back to 180°C/350°F (if the chicken fries in oil that is lower in temperature than this, it will become soggy and oily). The frying takes about 2–2½ minutes, you want the chicken to look crunchy and golden. Carefully remove the chicken pieces when done, and drain on a wire rack.

To serve, grind half and half of the salt and shichimi around your serving dish – it's great to dip the chicken in to. Get the chicken on the plate while it's still hot and serve the kimchi mayo and spicy shiso ponzu on the side, scattered with the chillies and lemon wedges to squeeze. Scull down with some sake, beer or shots.

SOMETHING CRUNCHY

GOBA TEMPURA IN KINOME SALT AND GRAPES

We don't serve a great deal of tempura dishes at Kurobuta. We don't copy the masses of Japanese-wanna-be joints that list every shitty, often out of season vegetable they can manage to think of and fry it in mass-produced glug, also referred to as batter, even tempura batter. To quote from *The Big Lebowski*, 'Your revolution is over.' It's not good enough to serve up total shit in fancy surroundings anymore. Why do I sound so cynical? Because here's the truth folks: this is exactly what happens, not always of course, but for the most part, the world over. It's junk, don't accept it.

Gobo is known in English as burdock and it's grown here in the UK. You often find it in dandelion and burdock drinks available in loads of places nowadays. Thinly cut gobo, dipped in this light batter and quickly fried makes an excellent snack. The flavour is distinct and earthy and doesn't require a dipping sauce - a little salt and lemon is all you need. Kinome is a tiny mega-fragrant green leafy herb from the sansho plant. Admittedly, it may be a struggle to find some, but there is a very cool couple growing this in East Sussex in the UK … go hunting for them! Alternatively, grab some sansho pepper.

SERVES 2, AS PART OF A LARGER SNACK SELECTION OR MULTI-COURSE MENU

a squeeze of lemon juice
20cm gobo
1 litre rapeseed oil, for deep-frying
20g plain flour, for dusting
60ml trisol batter (see page 251), chilled

For the kinome salt
6 sprigs kinome, or sansho pepper
2 tablespoons flaked sea salt, such
    as Maldon

To serve
flaked sea salt
2–3 grapes, halved
lemon wedges

Fill a bowl with water and add a squeeze of lemon. Peel and cut the gobo into 8–12cm lengths, then into fat matchsticks. Quickly drop them into the lemon water, otherwise they'll turn black quickly. Set aside.

Next, make the kinome salt. If you've managed to find, grow or steal some kinome then pick off the leaves and smash them up in a mortar and pestle with the sea salt. Refrigerate. Alternatively, if you're using the sansho pepper, put a few pinches into the salt, smash it up and it's good to go!

Just before you want to eat this, heat your fryer filled with spanking fresh rapeseed oil to 180°C/350°F. Drain the gobo from the lemon water, dry well on some kitchen paper, then lightly dredge in the flour. Shake to remove any excess.

Piece by piece, dip the gobo into the batter, then immediately into that nice hot glistening bath of oil. Deep-fry for about 2 minutes, until nicely golden and crunchy. Remove with a perforated spoon, drain on kitchen paper, and it's ready to serve up.

Arrange the crunchy gobo on a sheet of tempura paper (yeah, tempura has its own fancy paper! If you don't have any kicking about, print some naked photos of yourself and serve it on that, or not). The paper will soak up any excess oil. Place a little pile of the salt on the side and serve with the grapes and a freshly cut wedge of lemon.

LITTLE SHRIMP TEMPURA WITH KIMCHI AND KIMCHI MAYO

Do you remember when rock shrimp was as en-vogue as Harrods clothing or coked-up models? I do. It swept the planet like a plague of boy bands – you couldn't avoid it. I remember when I was asked to smuggle two large suitcases of frozen rock shrimp into Mykonos so they could feel the fashion. (Well, that was the 'naughties' and sustainability, MSC accreditation and shrimp-miles hadn't quite become as trendy as they needed to be.)

To be honest, I used to scoff my fair share of rock shrimp tempura, moreish little buggers they are. But something very similar can be created with similar small, plump shrimps, which are far more plentiful, as well as affordable. Here's my nod to that superstar of a dish.

SERVES 2 AS PART OF A MULTI-COURSE MENU

1 litre rapeseed oil, for deep-frying
120g small plump prawns, shells removed and deveined
15g tempura flour, for coating
70ml ice-cold trisol batter (see page 251)
salt

To serve
10g harusame noodles
30g kimchi pickle (see page 246)
25ml kimchi mayo (see page 246)
¼ small red onion, thinly sliced, rinsed and drained well
1 teaspoon chopped chives
10 slices green chilli

Heat the oil in a fryer or large pan to 180°C/350°F. Add the noodles and deep-fry for a few seconds, until crisp and nicely puffed. Remove with a perforated scoop and drain on a plate lined with kitchen paper.

Mix about 10 per cent salt to water (around 30g salt to 300ml water) and wash the prawns in the salty water. Drain well.

If you've let it cool down, crank the oil in a fryer or large pan back to 180°C/350°F, and toss the prawns in the tempura flour, shaking to coat well. Place the prawns in a colander and shake off the excess flour.

Next, drop the prawns into the ice-cold batter, one by one, and, by hand, coat each in the batter. Working quickly, drop the prawns individually into the hot oil, spacing them well apart. Cook for about 2½ minutes until nice and golden (traditionally tempura is much paler but this batter won't work if we try to cook it less to try and achieve the pale colour – besides, these little nuggets will be crunchier than the pale stuff). Remove the prawns with a perforated scoop and allow to drain well in a colander.

Arrange your crunchy harusame noodles on a suitable plate – I use a shallow bowl so they don't slide around when being rushed from the kitchen to the table. Dot kimchi over the plate, top with the crunchy prawns, drizzle with the kimchi mayo (best done using a squeezy bottle with a thin nozzle), then scatter with the red onion, chives and chilli slices.

Eat quickly and be merry!

SQUID KARA-AGE WITH YELLOW CHILLI DRESSING

OK, firstly let's clear up some common confusion with the term 'kara-age'. It often gets confused with 'kaki-age', probably because both have the word 'age' (pronounced a-geh) in the name, which refers to the dish being fried. As far as I can tell, Westerners seem to be far more familiar with kara-age than kaki-age, so receiving kaki-age when you thought you'd ordered kara-age could leave you a little dazed and confused. Let's finally clear this up. Kara-age is when an ingredient (most popular being chicken) is fried in seasoned flour or other plain starch. Kaki-age is when various ingredients are combined with tempura batter and fried in clusters, sometimes large, sometimes small, and these are more refined. Enough of that, let's recipe...

This dish is always eaten hard and fast so make plenty!

SERVES 2 AS PART OF A MULTI-COURSE MENU

80g small baby squid
1 litre rapeseed oil, for deep-frying
½ lime, cut into wedges, to serve

For the yellow chilli dressing

1 yellow pepper
3 long yellow chillies, plus a few extra
   to serve
3 garlic cloves, crushed
50ml Japanese rice vinegar
1 tablespoon lemon juice
1 teaspoon green Tabasco
a large pinch of katsuobushi
   (bonito flakes)
a pinch of sea salt
150ml grapeseed oil

For the daikon pickle garnish

¼ large daikon
50ml Japanese rice vinegar
30g caster sugar
a large pinch of sea salt
1 teaspoon grated yuzu zest or lemon
   zest, optional
1 dried chilli, optional
3cm piece kombu, optional

For the seasoned flour

150g tempura flour
1 tablespoon cayenne pepper
1 tablespoon shichimi togarashi
1 tablespoon finely ground black pepper
½ tablespoon fine sea salt

First, make the yellow chilli dressing. Put the yellow pepper and chillies directly on the gas hob over a medium-high flame, or over hot coals on a BBQ, and scorch for 5–6 minutes, until the skin is burnt or scorched and flaky. Use metal tongs to turn them around occasionally. Remove from the heat and allow to cool. Peel away the black skin and roughly chop the soft, smoky flesh, seeds and all. Small black specks of charred skin are fine, too. Put the pepper and chilli flesh in a food processor with the remaining dressing ingredients, except the oil, and blend until very smooth. Now, with the motor running, slowly drizzle the oil into the processor, drop by drop, until emulsified. Decant into a glass jar and store in the refrigerator where it will keep for 1 week.

To make the daikon pickle, peel away the outer skin of the daikon, then use a mandoline to shave about 20 slices (if you don't have a mandoline, just slice the daikon as thinly as possible – about 2mm). Next, put the rice vinegar, sugar and salt in a pan and place over a medium heat. Cook, undisturbed, for 1 minute, until the sugar and salt have dissolved. Remove from the heat and pour the mixture over the daikon slices. Too simple? You can add some yuzu zest and dried chilli to the vinegar mixture when you heat it up. Love umami too? Add a small 3cm square of kombu whilst warming.

Next, prepare the squid. Cut open the squid tubes and lie them flat. Use a sharp knife to score the flesh of the inside of the tubes. Cut each tube in half. You want small, bite-sized pieces that are manageable with chopsticks, so if the squid is on the larger size, cut it into smaller chunks.

To make the seasoned flour, mix all the ingredients by hand. If you have any left, store in an airtight container and it will probably keep for future generations. It's great used for chicken kara-age or just more squid, or use the same method as noted here with small chunks or strips of chicken or cubes of tofu.

Heat your spanking fresh oil for deep-frying in a fryer or a large pan to 195°C/380°F. Working in batches, massage your prepared squid with a generous, even coating of the seasoned flour making sure you get into every nook and cranny. When you think you're done, do it again and then sprinkle more seasoned flour over the top. Carefully drop into the hot oil. The squid will cook super-fast, and should be done in around 1 minute. Remove immediately when mildly coloured and drain on a wire rack before transferring to kitchen paper to drain completely.

PUMPKIN TEMPURA

A pretty basic idea, right? You may have even tried small pieces of pumpkin tempura in Japanese restaurants before. However, we are going to turbo charge this fucker. It's too easy (and usually as boring as hell) to dip some average lacklustre vegetable in some sludgy excuse for a batter then fry it. I've had enough of that circus food – here's a tasty, crunchy bastard that is actually great to eat. The pumpkin gets roasted with some umami-rich additions. It gets cooled down and then fried in the mega-crunchy trisol batter – soft and damn tasty in the middle with the ultimate crunchy exterior. Screw traditions, crunchy rules, bitches!

SERVES 2 AS PART OF A MULTI-COURSE MENU

1 litre rapeseed oil, for deep-frying
tempura flour, for dusting
200ml trisol batter (see page 251)

For the roast pumpkin

2 wedges best-quality squash or pumpkin
  (make sure it has an edible skin, such
  as the Japanese varieties), cut to
  around 2cm thick at the thickest part
  (around 175g total)
1 tablespoon salted capers, rinsed
  and drained
2 anchovy fillets
a large pinch of katsuobushi
  (bonito flakes)
2 tablespoons dark soy sauce
2 garlic cloves, crushed
1 teaspoon shichimi togarashi
2 tablespoons sake
30g butter, diced

For the pickled pumpkin

25ml Japanese rice vinegar
15g caster sugar
a pinch of sea salt
50g pumpkin, cut into 5–6cm long
  julienne strips

To serve

½ recipe spicy shiso ponzu (see
  page 249)
50ml Japanese Kewpie mayonnaise

First, make the roast pumpkin. Preheat the oven to 180°C/160°C fan/Gas Mark 4. Combine all the ingredients so that the pumpkin is fairly well coated. Wrap in an aluminium foil parcel and bake for around 30–35 minutes, or until the pumpkin is roasted at the edges and tender. (The time will vary depending on the pumpkin variety, but be careful and check regularly.) Remove from the oven and allow the pumpkin to cool completely in the foil parcel, then refrigerate until required.

Next, mix the spicy shiso ponzu with the mayonnaise in a bowl and set aside while you make the pickled pumpkin. Combine the vinegar, sugar and salt in a saucepan and place over a medium heat for about 2 minutes, or until the sugar and salt have dissolved. Pour over the pumpkin strips and leave to pickle for at least 30 minutes. Transfer to the refrigerator and chill before serving.

Getting ready to rock… Heat the oil in a fryer or large pan to 180°C/350°F.

Remove the roasted pumpkin from the refrigerator and brush off any capers from the pumpkin pieces. Lightly dredge the pumpkin with the flour, then dip into the batter and coat well. Carefully lower the pumpkin pieces into the hot oil and cook for 1½ minutes, or until golden.

To serve, cut the pumpkin wedges in half and arrange on your sexiest tempura plate with the ponzu mayonnaise and pickled pumpkin in a dipping cup on the side.

JERUSALEM ARTICHOKE CHOPSTICKS WITH TRUFFLE PONZU

Chopsticks: a fancy new name for a kind of spring roll, or, as they are known in Japan, harumaki. I used to make these little crackers with a filling made from lightly curried Japanese mushrooms but I was out one day mountain biking and I went flying head first into a tree, at a rather high speed - I was concussed for weeks. It was at that time that I wondered how good the crackers would taste filled with Jerusalem artichokes and truffles. That bump on the head did me good - it's brilliant, but

unfortunately the mushrooms had to find another gig. Make a load of these chopsticks and freeze 'em up. They defrost quickly and fry to a golden crunch in moments, making you look like the master of instant awesomeness when unannounced mo-fos drop in to drink all your booze.

You can buy the pastry online or from specialist shops. If you are really desperate you *could* use spring roll pastry but I'll warn you now it will be total crap in comparison and you will cry.

MAKES ABOUT 20

For the filling
60ml light olive oil
1 small white onion, diced
3 garlic cloves, finely chopped
1 teaspoon ground cumin
500g Jerusalem artichokes
lemon wedge, for the artichokes
500ml dry white wine
2 litres dashi (see page 245)
truffle oil, to taste
6 spring onions, finely chopped
50g pickled ginger, finely chopped
sea salt and freshly ground black pepper

For the chopsticks
10 sheets feuilles de brick pastry
2 tablespoons cornflour mixed with 2
  tablespoons water, to form a paste
1 litre vegetable oil, for deep-frying
chopped chives, to serve, optional

For the truffle ponzu
100ml Japanese mayonnaise
40ml ponzu sauce (see page 247)
1 tablespoon lemon juice
½ teaspoon truffle oil, to taste

Equipment
disposable piping bag

First make the filling. Heat the oil in a pan and sauté your onions, garlic and cumin over a low heat until very soft. Do it slowly, for at least 10 minutes, taking your time in order to build a solid flavour base.

Meanwhile, peel and roughly chop the artichokes and put them in a bowl of water with a wedge of lemon until you're ready to cook with them (this will stop them from going brown).

When the onions are really soft, drain the chopped artichokes and add them to the pan. Stir to coat them well with the onion mix and sauté over a medium heat for 3 minutes. Add the wine and turn up the heat and allow the liquid to reduce for about 8 minutes, until almost dry. Next, add the dashi, cover the pan and cook for 45–50 minutes; the artichokes need to be nice and soft and the liquid cooked out. Remove from the heat and season with truffle oil, salt and pepper and the chopped spring onions and ginger. Allow to cool completely, then transfer to a container or bowl and refrigerate.

Once chilled, spoon the artichoke mix into a disposable piping bag and cut the pointy end off to leave an 8mm hole. Set aside while you prepare the pastry.

Cut the pastry sheets in half so that you end up with 20 half-moon sheets. Keep them under a damp tea towel while you work. Take a pastry sheet, one at a time, and position it with the straight edge facing you and the round edge facing away. Use a pastry brush to brush the whole sheet with a little of the cornflour mix.

To make the 'chopsticks' pipe a long solid line of the artichoke mix parallel to the straight edge, leaving 1cm from the edge. Now, starting at the straight edge, begin rolling the pastry around the artichoke mix. When you get to the curved end, paint a little of the cornflour mix onto the pastry and roll to seal. Place the chopstick on a sheet of baking parchment and continue making the rest. Refrigerate or freeze as soon as possible. These can be stored in the refrigerator for up to 3 days or frozen for up to 2 weeks.

When you're just about ready to serve, make the truffle ponzu. Mix together all the ingredients and set aside.

Heat the vegetable oil in a fryer or large pan to 180°C/350°F. Deep-fry the chopsticks 2 or 3 at a time for about 2 minutes, or until golden. Remove to drain on a wire rack before transferring to kitchen paper to drain completely. To serve, cut in half and have the truffle ponzu on the side, sprinkled with the chopped chives.

TEBASAKI GYOZA

In Japan, tebasaki gyoza refers to a chicken wing that has been stuffed, and sometimes crumbed, then fried. You could use gyoza (dumpling) filling as the stuffing. I got to thinking about these crunchy bandits, and being trained in French technique initially as an apprentice, I still revert to thinking about the way of the French from time to time. I made a confit with the wings, removed the bones then crumbed them, but that wasn't the kind of crunch I wanted. So with French nuttiness on the brain I decided to use feuilles de brick pastry, which despite its name hails from North Africa, or so they say. Anyway, brick was a winner – it kind of loosely resembles gyoza but most importantly it tastes fantastic.

For a tapas or starters portion you only need a few wings but I'd recommend making a larger batch in advance as they keep well.

SERVES 2 AS PART OF A MULTI-COURSE MENU

2 sheets feuilles de brick pastry
1 tablespoon cornflour mixed with 2 tablespoons water, to form a paste
olive oil, for shallow frying

For the chicken confit
6 corn-fed chicken wings
300g chicken skins
7cm piece kombu
2cm piece ginger, sliced
3 garlic cloves, crushed
3 star anise
sea salt

To serve
a pinch of Japanese sesame seeds
a pinch of sea salt
spicy Korean miso (see page 249)

First, prepare the chicken wings. You only want the middle section so cut off the tip and the bit that connects the wing to the bird. Season the wings with salt, and refrigerate for 1½ hours.

Meanwhile, render some chicken fat for the confit. Place the chicken skins, 4cm of kombu and a large pinch of salt into a large deep pan, and pour over enough cold water to come up to just below the surface of the chicken skins. Cut a sheet of baking parchment to the size of the pan and place it on top of the chicken skins, just touching the surface. Set the pan over a medium heat and allow it to cook gently for about 40 minutes, until golden and crunchy. Remove the pan from the heat, strain while still hot (being very careful) into a bowl and discard the solids.

Preheat the oven to 60°C/40°C fan/Gas Mark very low. (If your oven doesn't go this low, use a pan on the hob to cook the wings, checking the temperature with a thermometer. You can adjust the heat in order to maintain the optimum temperature, but a little higher or lower won't be the end of the world.)

Take the wings out of the refrigerator and wipe away the salt. Arrange the wings in a deep roasting tray, then pour over the rendered fat. Add a few slices of ginger, the remaining 3cm of kombu, the garlic cloves and star anise. Cover the tray with foil and cook in the oven for 4 hours. Remove from the oven and leave the wings to cool in the chicken fat. If you're not using the wings immediately, store in an airtight container, with the fat, in the refrigerator where they will keep for up to 5 days.

When ready for your wings, you need to remove them from the fat and carefully push the bones out – they should pop out quite easily. Trim away any excess cartilage from the ends of the wing and pat dry to remove any excess fat with kitchen paper.

Time to wrap them up …

Take a sheet of the pastry and cut 3 strips around 6cm wide. (Because this pastry comes in rounds, each strip will be a different length.) Stack the strips on top of each other then trim the ends so that they are more or less the same length – you should end up with strips that are around 18cm long. Repeat with the remaining sheet of pastry until you have 6 strips.

recipe continued on page 94

Take 1 strip of pastry per wing and brush with a little of the cornflour paste. Place a wing at one end of the pastry and roll to create several layers of pastry. Brush a little more cornflour paste on the join and seal well. Repeat with the remaining pastry and wings, then put them on a tray lined with baking parchment and refrigerate immediately.

To cook, heat the oil in a large pan and shallow fry the gyozas over a medium-high heat for 1½ minutes on each side, or until crunchy and golden. You can fry these ahead of any guests arriving and reheat them in the oven preheated to 190°C/170°C fan/Gas Mark 5 for about 4 minutes.

Crunch the sesame seeds with the sea salt in a mortar and pestle until roughly ground. Serve the gyozas hot with some spicy Korean miso and the sesame-salt mixture sprinkled over the top. Hey yeah!

CREAMY SWEETCORN CROQUETTES IN BROWN CRAB AIOLI (AKA KRABBY PATTIES)

Corn and crab seem to be pretty good mates. To me, this is another way of approaching a 'surf 'n' turf'. This dish came about when I was watching *SpongeBob SquarePants* with my kids. It's a cool concept: there is a giant crab whose restaurant's USP is these legendary krabby patties. They look like hamburgers to me. I'm not sure whether they are your usual mystery-meat burger patties or he's murdering his fellow crabs and turning them into patties. Whatever the case, it's all mystical underwater fun, nothing really needs a reason. So Jack, my eldest boy, says, 'Dad, you should serve krabby patties in your restaurants.' He was so right, what a great idea! I thought, croquettes are so popular in Japan, why not make that the basis of my very own patties. I wanted the crabbiness to be up front and in your face, so I made an aioli with brown crabmeat (Japanese folk call this 'kani miso') then drizzled it over some sweet, sweetcorn croquettes. There you have krabby patties, Kurobuta style.

Soundtrack: at the end of one of the *SpongeBob* films they play 'Ocean Man' by Ween, it's a must whilst you prep this dish!

SERVES 2 AS PART OF A MULTI-COURSE MENU

For the croquettes (makes about 12 pieces, they freeze well so you don't need to be concerned about having any waste)

3 corncobs, husks removed
10g unsalted butter
a squeeze of lemon juice
a dash of soy sauce
15g white crabmeat (not from a can!)
25g brown crabmeat (not from a can!)
35g king crabmeat
50g béchamel sauce (see page 244)
40g cooked and mashed potatoes
15g spring onions, chopped
15g sushi gari, chopped
40g plain flour, for dusting
1 egg, beaten
approx. 150g Japanese panko
    breadcrumbs
a pinch of sea salt and freshly ground
    black pepper

For the brown crab aioli

½ teaspoon garlic purée
zest of ½ lemon
1 teaspoon S&B Japanese mustard
    powder
2 egg yolks
½ tablespoon yuzu kosho (yuzu pepper
    paste)
a generous pinch of sea salt
1 tablespoon lemon juice
½ tablespoon low-sodium soy sauce
110g brown crabmeat
115ml grapeseed oil

First make the croquettes. Heat a grill pan and char the corncobs over a high heat, until nicely coloured. Take off the heat and toss in a whack of butter, squeeze of lemon juice and splash of soy sauce, whilst still hot. Cover with clingfilm and allow to cool. Cut the kernels from the cob and put half in a food processor or blender to purée until smooth. Mix both the whole corn kernels and puréed corn in a bowl; add the crabmeat, béchamel sauce, mashed potato, spring onion and sushi gari and season with salt and pepper. Chill for 45 minutes to firm the mixture up.

Form the mixture into 20–30g hamburger patties, using flour-dusted hands to shape them. Chill again for at least 30 minutes.

While the patties are chilling, make your brown crab aioli. Whack all the ingredients, except the oil, in a blender or food processor, and blitz well until really smooth. Slowly drizzle in the grapeseed oil, until the mixture has thickened. If it appears too thick for your liking, just drizzle in a little hot water. Go get 'em!

When the patties are nicely chilled, coat them in the flour, then dip them into some beaten egg followed by the breadcrumbs. Chill or freeze your patties again at this point for at least 10 minutes.

When it's krabby time, set up your fryer with clean oil and heat the oil to 180°C/350°F. When the oil is at temperature, carefully drop the patties (in batches if necessary) into the hot oil and fry for 2½ minutes. Check if they are done by sticking a metal skewer or thin, small knife into the centre of one of the patties to check if it's totally cooked and hot all the way through. If not, continue to fry for another minute, then remove using a perforated scoop.

Drain well on kitchen paper and serve with a massive dollop of brown crab aioli, or, get the aioli into a squeezy bottle and get artistic, squirting it all over your patties.

ANAGO TEMPURA WITH STICKY STAR ANISE SAUCE

As far as popular Japanese eel dishes go, unagi kabayaki, the sweet, grilled freshwater eel, takes centre stage. You'll see it teamed with its good mates - various sushi preparations or donburi - or going it solo with a side of extra sweet, sticky soy and sansho pepper. Anago, salt water eel, could be thought of as the red-headed stepchild of the eel. It's just as good, but it still sits in the shadow of its rock star relation, unagi.

So let's pimp our anago. Buy it pre-grilled from Japanese food shops - don't substitute it with some other weird shit like English jellied eels or that smoky stuff those nuts, the Dutch, make. This recipe is for anago. The recipe for the sauce will make more than you need, but I'd recommend making the full batch as it will keep in the fridge until the end of time. Plus, it's great to barbecue chicken with, drizzle over maki rolls or, if you lose your marbles, drizzle over your cornflakes. Along with the sticky star anise sauce, this dish is quite rich, so serve it as part of a tapas feast.

Serves 2 as part of a 7–8 plate tapas feast

1 litre rapeseed oil, for deep-frying
120g anago, cut into 5–6cm strips,
   1–1½cm thick
tempura flour, for dusting
200ml ice-cold trisol batter (see
   page 251)

For the sticky star anise sauce
400ml sake
370ml mirin
370ml light soy sauce
2 tablespoons tamari
65g caster sugar
6 pieces star anise, toasted in a dry pan

To serve
4cm piece daikon, finely shredded
½ medium carrot, finely shredded
¼ large cucumber, finely shredded
small knob ginger, finely grated
½ lime, cut into wedges
sansho pepper, to sprinkle

First make the sauce by combining the ingredients in a small saucepan. Mix well, place over a very low heat and cook gently for 1 hour, until thickened. Don't allow the mixture to boil as this will result in an astringent sauce. Be very patient. Set aside while you prepare the rest of the dish.

Put the finely shredded daikon, carrot and cucumber in ice-cold water to cover and leave for 1 hour to get them nice and crisp.

Next, heat enough clean oil for deep-frying in a fryer or large pan to 180°C/350°F. Lightly dust your anago strips with tempura flour and shake off the excess. In ice-cold batter, dip in the anago, piece by piece, then gently swish it into the hot oil. Flick a little extra batter over the frying strips of anago for some extra crunchy goodness and let these little buggers fry for around 2 minutes, until nice and golden. And yes, purists, you're absolutely right, traditional tempura is never 'golden' in appearance. Traditional tempura is also never crunchy, and I'm into the crunch, enough said. When done, put the fried anago on a wire rack and transfer to tempura paper (or kitchen paper), which will absorb any excess oil.

Drain the finely shredded vegetables well.

To serve, place your anago together with a small mound of the grated ginger, lime and the finely shredded vegetables on a plate. Sprinkle the whole plate lightly with sansho pepper. Remove the star anise from the sauce and serve (at room temperature) on the side.

BBQ AND
FIRE PITS

FIRE PIT QUAIL

Quail rhymes with baby whale! 'So what?' you may ask. Well, I'll tell you. As a (sometimes) mischievous young chef, my fellow chefs and I used to take great pleasure in confusing the waiters as best we could. On one particular occasion we assured one of them that the special of the day was pan-roasted baby whale. That particular waiter was well aged and possibly had a few screws loose so she totally went for it.

She went ahead and told all of the waiters who gave different reactions: anger, laughter, confusion and even belief! We managed to get a few more miles out of that one until it was finally banned. Not to worry, there are hundreds of kitchen pranks to work with - that very same waiter was also led to believe that we were keeping a pet cat in the kitchen. I thought, hang on, she's just playing along with the gag, even when we left bowls of milk out for it. Apparently not - eventually she told the boss about it and, just like that, our imaginary cat was gone forever!

Anyway, back to the recipe... here is some sweet, smoky quail, roasted over cedar and charcoal.

SERVES 2

2 quail

40ml sake

2 spring onions, roughly chopped, plus
    a little extra

4cm piece ginger, roughly chopped, plus
    a little extra

4cm piece kombu, plus a little extra

steamed rice, to serve

For the teriyaki glaze

1 part sake

1 part mirin

1 part dark soy sauce

½ part caster sugar

Make the glaze by warming the ingredients over a gentle heat to dissolve the sugar. Cool and chill.

Prepare the quail by trimming the wing tips and removing the innards if not already done. Rinse with sake and drain away the sake.

Put the quail in a bowl and pour half the teriyaki glaze into its cavity, swish it about, then stuff with the spring onion, ginger and kombu. The liquid will leak a little, save what you can of it.

Get a fire going using some charcoal and cedarwood, if you can get it. If not, then stick with just the charcoal, you will just miss out on the extra smokiness. Let the fire die down so that you have red-hot glowing embers.

Place the quail on a sheet of foil with a few extra pieces of spring onion, ginger, kombu and the remaining teriyaki sauce. Wrap it all up and bury it in the charcoal and wood embers. It will take around 20 minutes to slowly cook through.

Remove your package, and, using tongs, carefully open up the foil package and see how it's getting on – if the leg pulls away from the body easily, the quail is cooked. If there is some resistance, wrap it up again and bury it in the embers for a few more minutes.

I'd suggest you open up your little barbecued quail bomb and dump it out onto a deep plate, sauce and all, then get stuck in with your fingers. I highly recommend some hot, freshly steamed rice to soak up those sweet, smoky juices.

TEA-SMOKED LAMB WITH SPICY KOREAN MISO

I grew up eating lamb chops from the barbecue. For as long as I can remember, lamb chops always featured on most people's 'barbies' where I came from. The best, most moreish thing about barbecued lamb chops is when the fatty part becomes golden, verging on charred or slightly crunchy. So, this version was born out of a yearning for the chops from my childhood. I needed to get some smoky barbecue attributes without overcooking the meat (like we used to at home) enter the smoking process…

Using Japanese sencha with my woodchips was a natural choice, which worked perfectly. I've tried it with other Japanese teas such as genmai cha and matcha, and both work brilliantly, but the sencha seemed to be received the best in the restaurant. This smoking technique can be used for other ingredients such as prawns, salmon belly, scallops or chicken. Before you get stuck into smoking your chops, you'll need to marinate them. For ours we are adding some umami (that secret wallop of flavour that turns you from a backyard barbecue nobody to the 'Holy Shit' barbecue boss). Secondly the salt in the marinade helps the meat to take on the smoke - yep, somehow that's true!

Never been a smoker? Don't worry, it's pretty straightforward. You don't really need any fancy kit either: an old wok, a wire cake rack or something similar, something to cover the wok with (a plate, bowl or ugly hat) and you're off and racing!

SERVES 4

8 plump lamb chops
½ tablespoon rapeseed oil
spicy Korean miso (see page 249)
sea salt and freshly ground black pepper

For the lamb cure mix

½ red onion, roughly chopped
2 garlic cloves
2cm piece ginger
1 long red chilli
a small handful of coriander stems
    and roots
20g sea salt

For the smoke mix

50g fine smoking chips
70g uncooked rice
35g sencha green tea leaves

First make the cure mix. You can do this a day or so in advance. Blitz all the ingredients together in a food processor until fine. Coat the lamb in the mix and allow it to marinate for 2 hours in the refrigerator.

After 2 hours, wipe the cure mix off the lamb chops. Line a wok or similar large pan with foil and then place it over a high heat and add in the wood chips. Once smoking, add the rice and heat through, then add the green tea.

Place the lamb chops on a rack and place over the smoke, covering well. Hot smoke f or 2 minutes on each side.

Remove the lamb chops from the heat and set aside for at least a couple of hours to allow the harsh astringent smokiness to mellow. Chill until required.

When you're ready to cook the lamb chops, rub each one lightly with a little oil and season with some sea salt and freshly ground black pepper.

Heat a ridged grill pan until searingly hot. Chargrill the lamb chops for about 2½ minutes on each side – it should be cooked on the outside but pink on the inside. Serve with the spicy Korean miso on the side.

SLOW-COOKED BARBECUED PORK BELLY WITH RED MISO SAUCE

Slow cooked this, slow cooked that – it's mentioned all over the place these days, and it's almost a bit too trendy for my liking. Bah humbug you might say. It's not that I'm not into it. I clearly am. It may just be a case of, sometimes, false advertising: the term 'slow cooking' thrown about by foodies (another annoying term of our times) and chefs to evoke feelings of passion and lovingly cooked food when it isn't always accurate.

If you're cooking 'low and slow', as it's often called in North America, you need to be down with your temperatures and timings. Experimenting is one way to go. It's really fun and can lead to great results. No time for that malarkey? You could always look up Harold McGee or type into the Google machine, or check this out. Follow the recipe closely – it will be spot on.

The whole purpose of slow cooking is to break down the tough connective tissue of the meat until it's soft and gelatinous at the same time as not overcooking the more vulnerable meat fibres. It can be a tricky balancing act, but one that comes with a whole load of fun as you experiment heaps and pig out on the results.

Do not attempt this with cheap and lacklustre pork. Make an effort to find a good breed such as Gloucester Old Spot or the Berkshire pig, one that has been farmed with care. This isn't about being all 'cheffy', it makes a shit-ton of difference to the end dish. You can cook the pork and chill it a couple of days ahead of when you plan to serve it.

SERVES 2 AS PART OF A MULTI-COURSE MENU

2kg good-quality pork belly

For the cure mix
1 teaspoon Sichuan peppercorns
100g fine sea salt
2 small dried red chillies (if they are killer-hot, deseed)
55g soft brown sugar
10cm piece kombu, broken into small pieces

For the slow-cook mix
2 litres dashi (see page 245)
200ml sake
200ml mirin
200ml dark soy sauce
5cm piece kombu
1cm slice ginger

For the red miso sauce
1 tablespoon sake
1 tablespoon mirin
55g caster sugar
100g red miso paste

First, toast the Sichuan peppercorns in a small dry pan over a medium heat until aromatic. Remove and put in a clean, dry blender or spice grinder with the remaining ingredients for the cure. Blitz together until fine.

Next, rub the pork belly all over with the cure mix, then cover with clingfilm and refrigerate for 1 hour.

Take the pork belly out of the fridge and rinse away the cure mix with cold running water, drain well.

Combine all the ingredients for the slow-cook mix in a bowl and pour into a large vacuum-pack plastic bag, along with the cured pork belly. Carefully seal and suck out as much air as possible. Alternatively, if you're the type of person who like things a little more low-tech, then simply put the pork belly in a large roasting tray and cover entirely with the slow-cook mixture; the trick will be to find an ovenproof tray that will allow for both the pork and this amount of liquid. Clingfilm it well, maybe even twice, then cover twice with foil.

Now, we have two possible ways to proceed. This part gets a bit like those Pick-a-Path books…

Option 1: If you have an oven that will allow you to cook using 50 per cent steam and 50 per cent convection, crank it up to 85°C/65°C fan, put the pork in and set your timer to 8½ hours.

Option 2: If you have a basic oven, crank that up to 110°C/90°C fan/Gas Mark ¼ and place another roasting tray, filled with water, on the bottom shelf. Get your pork tray

ingredients continued on page 108

recipe continued on page 108

To serve

½ Granny Smith apple

roasted cashew nuts, chopped, optional

in there to cook for about 7 hours. It's hard to judge perfectly as ovens are not always calibrated properly. If it's not lovely and soft when you press a fork into it, keep the pork cooking and keep checking.

Once the cooking is complete, cool the pork as quickly as possible. Baggers can fill the sink with ice and water and really get it chilled down mega-fast. Tray lovers can take the pork out and cool it on a wire rack. Once cooled, refrigerate for a good 2 hours to get it really chilled before cutting away the rind, then portion into 10cm x 3cm pieces. At this stage, the pork can be kept in the fridge for up to 3 days if you want to prep it in advance of serving.

To make the miso sauce, combine the sake, mirin and sugar in a saucepan and bring to the boil. Whisk in the red miso and cook for about 30 seconds, until well combined. Remove from the heat and cool.

The next part is almost effortless, so if you've done all your homework, you'll look pretty slick when you whip it out in front of your future fans!

Either get that charcoal cranked up and barbecue the porky portions over the glowing hot charcoal (let any flames die down so that you have a super-hot, even charcoal base), until well coloured. Alternatively, heat up a little oil in a frying pan and sear the pork over a medium-high heat until you have golden porky goodness.

Once well coloured, chop your porky chunks into 3–4 pieces so that they can be easily managed with chopsticks.

Smear some of the red miso sauce onto your serving dish, top with your porky bits then grate the apple (leaving the skin on) and make a little pile on the plate. I'd recommend some chopped roasted cashews scattered over the lot as well.

MAKIN' BACON

Bacon isn't the kind of ingredient that springs to mind when you start thinking about Japanese food. It is, however, one of the first items that jumps out at me on an izakaya menu. Asparagus or scallops wrapped in bacon then grilled over glowing charcoal with a soy-mirin glaze are as part of the Japanese izakaya as anything else. You'll even see it offered in okonomiyaki.

I was pretty stoked to discover this when I first visited Tokyo. I returned to London with makin' bacon on my mind. I wanted to make use of Japanese ingredients, not just come up with a nice bacon. Kombu was the first, most obvious inclusion. Pork belly needs to be brined before it is hung to mature (and sometimes smoked). The kombu was going to make this bacon worth fucking about with. (Kombu is like a secret weapon - seriously, it's some gourmet shit!)

The recipe makes more cure than you need for but make it all and store it - it lasts for ages. We sometimes use the cure for salting Chinese cabbage before making it into Kurobuta-style kimchi (as an alternative to the one on page 246).

MAKES 800G BACON

1kg boneless pork belly (rind is fine
   to leave on)

**For the cure (enough for a 2kg
pork, see introduction above)**
1kg fine salt
80g toasted Sichuan peppercorns
30g dried red chillies (I use Japanese
   taka-no-tsume chillies)
570g dark brown sugar
20cm piece kombu

Equipment
2 nice big sheets of muslin (enough
   to triple wrap the pork belly)

To make the cure, blend all the ingredients in a spice grinder until fine. Put on some gloves and rub the pork belly vigorously with the cure mix. Massage, caress and finish it off by adding an extra layer of the mix. The idea is that it needs to be really well rubbed in as well as having a nice coating.

Wrap the pork belly up neatly and tightly with the muslin and tie it up with the kitchen string, like you were wrapping a bow around a box. Hang it from a shelf in your fridge for 3½ days. It's really important that when the bacon hangs it isn't touching anything. If it does, it can attract a build up of moisture, which leads to spoilage. The aim here is to allow it to dry out and let it continue to cure so that the flavours develop.

Unwrap, rinse off the cure and dry well with a paper towel or tea towel. Rewrap as before in fresh muslin. Now for the long wait. Hang once again from a shelf in your fridge for 2 weeks – you'll have yourself some bacon!

When it's time to use, cut carefully into long bacon-like slices. Use up the trimmings in stir-fries, risottos, or fry until crunchy and blend it into a big, fat, porky homemade mayonnaise.

ASPARA-BACON KUSHI

If you've never tried bacon, I mean real bacon from a pig (not turkey, veal or tofu bacon), I feel bad for you, genuinely. I regret the fact that religion or diet choice had a part to play in why there are many who haven't loved this product before, but it is so damn good, salty, sometimes smoky, sometimes crunchy, always full of umami (except for watery cheap shit, don't even go near it), always a joy to add to risotto, wrap over chicken or scallops, sandwich between bread, the list goes on...

Not traditionally Japanese, bacon is a super-common ingredient in a kushyaki, or okonomiyaki bar. Aspara-bacon, literally asparagus and bacon skewers, is something I can never avoid.

You won't really need much by way of accompaniment, just a light drizzle of some sweet, sticky soy sauce would be spot on.

Do not attempt this with imposter bacon – veal, turkey or whatever else is sacrilegiously used to impersonate the real deal – there is no substitute for bacon awesomeness. Wanna make your own bacon? Check out page 111. It's not so difficult and well worth the effort.

Another thing, don't make this out of asparagus season; it is worth waiting until tasty, local stuff is available. In the UK, asparagus season is really short so get stuck into it as often as you can, while you can.

SERVES 2

6 asparagus spears
100g homemade bacon strips (see page 111), or any properly good bacon
a dash of oil
sweet soy sauce or lemon wedges, to serve

For the glaze
50ml mirin
50ml dark soy sauce

Mix the glaze in a spray bottle and set aside.

Peel the lower part of the asparagus – how high you go depends on how thick the outer skin is and how high up it goes. Eat a spear of asparagus and check where the tenderness finishes and you'll be able to tell how much of it needs peeling.

Wrap your strips of bacon around the asparagus, leaving the tips exposed.

Crank up your barbecue (you could do this in a frying pan but you'll miss out on one of the most important elements of this dish – the scorching way of the barbecue).

When you have a pit of mesmerising hot coals, gently stroke your asparagus with a little oil, then introduce them to the scorch.

Get out your spray bottle of mirin and soy, and give the asparagus a few bursts of glaze (be generous!) during the entire grilling process. Once the asparagus spears are nicely glazed and scorched from the barbie, whip them off and onto your serving plate.

A little sweet soy sauce is my favourite accompaniment, or you could serve them with lemon, salt and pepper. Crack open a frosty beer and get stuck in!

As you may well see from the photo, it's all
about grilling on sticks. In Japan, it's far more
complicated than my very basic description here.
The angle of the skewers and how many are used
is dependent on the ingredients, or how they are
cut. You have lengthways skewering (tate-gushi),
side skewering (yoko-gushi), flat skewering (hira-
gushi), and the list goes on.

KUSHIYAKI GRILLING

   I use two long skewers for the meat ones. This
simply holds them better: no escaping, meat! Also,
always soak your bamboo skewers in water for an
hour or so, this way they don't set alight when
you're grilling.

For the glaze, mix together 1 part soy to 1 part mirin and brush or spray all over your
sticks of goodness. (Fill a spray bottle and use this to spray your skewers as they cook.)

Grilling over hot charcoal is essential; kushiyaki grilling really shouldn't be done any
other way.

I want to keep it pretty basic, so here are some examples of the simple preparations that
we use, but it is worth having some fun with it, too.

Spicy sausage and spring onions: at the restaurant, we make a very garlicky,
spicy pork sausage and skewer it with spring onions.

Corn with spicy shiso ponzu (see page 249): cut the corn into 2cm-thick
chunks and glaze with ponzu.

Miso steak and white onions: marinate the steak in den miso (see page 244) for
a couple of hours before skewering with onions and grilling.

Boneless confit wings with spicy mayo: cut wings into individual joints and cook
at 55°C/130°F in duck fat with kombu and ginger for 12 hours – cool and remove the
bones then skewer and grill, serving with spicy mayo such as umami mayo (page 67)
or yuzo kosho mayo (page 251).

All of your ingredients should be given a slathering of the soy-mirin spray whilst grilling.
It's nice to serve a load of different sauces too: try spicy shiso ponzu (page 249), yellow
chilli dressing (page 82), kimchi mayo (page 246 – perfect with spicy sausage), chilli-
miso-truffle (page 173), spicy miso (page 64), spicy Korean miso (page 249).

YELLOWTAIL KAMAYAKI

This is an absolutely classic dish that everyone should try it at least once. When I first tried it, I was reluctant. It looks like some bone and skin from near the head of the fish with a little too much salt on. At that time, I had only just become a huge fan of all things sashimi and wasn't quite up for what looked like overcooked fish. I was handed a teaspoon and small pot of ponzu sauce; I'll never forget the creaminess, the slight saltiness and the amazing crunchy skin. I was yet again blown away and surprised by Japanese cuisine.

You can make this with salmon collar or the small fins near the belly of the salmon. The preparation is so damn easy I can't even provide a recipe. It's simply a matter of this...

SERVES 1 GREEDY BUGGER OR 2 SHARING-TYPE EATERS

1 whole yellowtail or salmon collar
sea salt, to sprinkle

To serve
40ml ponzu sauce (see page 247)
1 teaspoon finely grated daikon
    (tastes great and is really good for
    digestion, too)
a few lemon wedges

Ask your fishmonger (like we all have our own private fish dude, what a load of shit us chefs talk sometimes, I'll start again...) Find a fishmonger or fish supplier and ask for the yellowtail or salmon collar.

Make an X-shaped cut in the thickest, meatiest part of the collar. Preheat your grill – top heat is required here. Liberally sprinkle sea salt over the skin side of the collar, not on the underside.

Once your grill is hot, place the fish skin-side up and start cooking. It will take 12–15 minutes for the skin to begin to colour and blister.

Take off the heat and let the fish cool slightly. Stick a thin knife into the fleshiest part to check the temperature – if the knife blade is piping hot, the fish is ready.

Mix the ponzu with the daikon and serve together on the side with a wedge of lemon.

KOMBU-ROASTED CHILEAN SEA BASS

Roasting meat or fish on kombu is like flavour-cheating. Kombu is one of the top umami-rich ingredients. In short, umami-rich ingredients have large taste profiles, so, in this case, the kombu is simply adding tastiness. You may have heard about monosodium glutamate (MSG), basically a chemical seasoning famous in the Orient, which can instantly boost flavour with a very small pinch. I suppose this is the real flavour cheat.

MSG was developed by a Japanese professor - the very same professor who discovered and named umami - and it was his quick and easy chemical version that became a massive hit all over Asia. Anyway, don't go down the route of sprinkling that nasty stuff in your food - tastiness can be 'boosted' naturally with the likes of kombu, amongst plenty of other things.

Serves 2, as part of a multi-course menu

10cm piece kombu
40ml sake
150g slice Chilean sea bass (failing this, a firm oily fish or salmon belly will do)
2 small knobs of unsalted butter
spicy shiso ponzu (see page 249), to serve
sea salt and freshly ground black pepper

We cook this in a wood-fired oven at around 250°C but use an oven preheated to 240°C/220°C fan/Gas Mark 9 if you want.

Soak the kombu in the sake for 1 hour.

Drain the kombu and put it on a chopping board. Place the sea bass on the kombu, squash the butter on top and season with salt and pepper. Lift the assembly onto a roasting tray and cook for 10–12 minutes. This is the kind of fish that benefits from being well cooked – standard fish cooking rules don't apply here – it's done when you see the flesh beginning to flake nicely.

You can also cook it over charcoal on your barbecue. Set the fish onto the soaked kombu, as above, with the butter and seasoning, then place over moderately hot coals and put a stainless-steel bowl over the top. Depending on how hot your coals are, the fish should take about 15 minutes.

Serve the Chilean sea bass on the kombu with a generous dousing of spicy shiso ponzu (remind your diners that they shouldn't eat the kombu – we have guests giving it a shot quite often, despite the warning).

ROASTED SCALLOP WITH YUZU-TRUFFLE-EGG SAUCE AND YUZU TOBIKO

Eggs and their yolks are one of the most incredible ingredients ever. You can eat them cooked in various ways for breakfast, make ice cream, mayonnaise, polonaise, chop up boiled ones for sandwiches and, if you're mad enough, bury them until they're properly fucked up. What a wonderful ingredient! Me, I can't handle raw yolks. It's something I've tried to overcome many times but I still can't manage them. If I taste a slightly undercooked ice cream base I'll notice it. I've even fired somebody over it. Don't proclaim to know how to be a fucking pastry chef if you can't cook a proper ice cream base – because my weird problem with eggs will lead to you being caught out!

So, imagine when I had to taste a raw Japanese egg sauce that is basically whisked up yolks with seasonings. No fucking chance! The trouble is that it looks so damn good. All egg yolk preparations do. It's just that I'm cursed with not being able to tolerate the taste. The solution was easy. I could have these flavours and textures if I were to cook the egg yolk like a hollandaise sauce. I don't really care that it's not traditional, it works.

SERVES 2

1 fresh egg yolk
1 tablespoon sauce reduction (see below)
200ml clarified butter
1 teaspoon lemon juice
1 teaspoon yuzu juice
1½ teaspoons light soy sauce
white truffle oil, to taste
25g butter
a splash of olive oil
2 large diver scallops (or 4 smaller ones)
20g Japanese mushrooms, thinly sliced
   (whatever you have available – shiitake,
   oyster, shimeji, etc.)
8g yuzu tobiko (flying fish roe), to serve
sea salt and freshly ground black pepper

For the sauce reduction
1 small white onion, finely diced
2 thin slices ginger
150ml sake
150ml rice vinegar

First, make the sauce reduction by heating the ingredients in a pan over a medium heat. When it begins to bubble, turn the heat down to a simmer and allow to reduce by about three-quarters. Once reduced pour through a sieve and discard the solids.

In a bowl set over a pan of gently simmering water (make sure the bowl doesn't touch the water), whisk the egg yolk and 1 tablespoon of the reduction together vigorously, over a medium heat for 8 minutes, until the mixture becomes creamy and ribbon-like in consistency. Remove the bowl from the heat.

In a saucepan, melt the clarified butter and then gradually add to the egg-reduction mixture, in a slow trickle. Once the butter has been fully emulsified, add the lemon and yuzu juices, soy sauce and truffle oil, and season with sea salt to taste. Keep covered in a warm place until required.

Heat a non-stick pan and drop in a couple of blocks of good-quality butter (not emulsified veg oil shit that you picked up for half price – I mean butter, from cows) plus a splash of olive oil. Season your scallops with a little sea salt and freshly ground black pepper on both sides and, when the butter has melted and the pan is hot, add the scallops. Fry on one side only to begin with, until you have achieved a deep golden brown colour – this could take 2–3 minutes over a medium-high heat. Just prior to taking your golden beauties out of the pan, flip the scallops to given them a gentle warming on the yet-to-be-cooked side. Seriously, they only need 2 seconds then get them outta the pan!

In the same pan, whilst still hot, throw in some thinly sliced Japanese mushrooms. Cook for 1–2 minutes over a medium heat, until softened and a little coloured.

Time to plate up… Scallops onto the plate, top with the fried mushrooms, a large dollop-like drizzle of the sauce over the lot, then a scattering of yuzu tobiko.

Note: We use the following alternative garnishes in the restaurant: a scattering of hijiki (see page 41), or crispy renkon chips: slice fresh renkon (or lotus) on a mandoline, deep-fry in oil at 170°C/340°F, and then bake in a preheated oven on its lowest setting for 30 minutes to finish crisping.

LANGOUSTINES BAKED IN BARLEY MISO AND SAKE

This is one for the barbecue!

The langoustines get wrapped up in a double layer of foil and then nestled in the hot coals. I used to simply grill the langoustines, split in half, right on the grill bars - which is great, but I reckon you lose too much of the flavour. By cooking in the foil you retain all of the juices and you get to introduce the vapour of sake and meatiness of barley miso.

Barley miso is a chunky red miso, also known in Japan as moro (or moromi miso). It's commonly used as a condiment and is a total classic when a small dollop is served on a slice of cucumber. It's a pretty decent bar snack. Barley miso is a very good marinade for chicken thigh or salmon belly (see page 169). It's not the kind of miso that you would normally make miso soup from, but combined with some shiro miso, it works really well.

SERVES 2

6 langoustines, whole (cut lengthways through the middle, bash each claw to break it – you want easy access after cooking and it allows the flavours easy access, too)

40g barley miso

40ml sake

a pinch of flaked sea salt

Crank up the barbie.

Mix the langoustines in a bowl with the miso, sake and salt, then pour on top of a double layer of foil. Wrap it up tightly, squishing the edges and doing your best to ensure there are no holes.

Nestle the langoustines into the hot barbecue coals and cook for 10–15 minutes (very hot coals will take 10 minutes, weak coals, or not enough coals, will take longer).

Pour the cooked langoustines (along with any juices) into a bowl and feast! (Don't forget to drink the juices.)

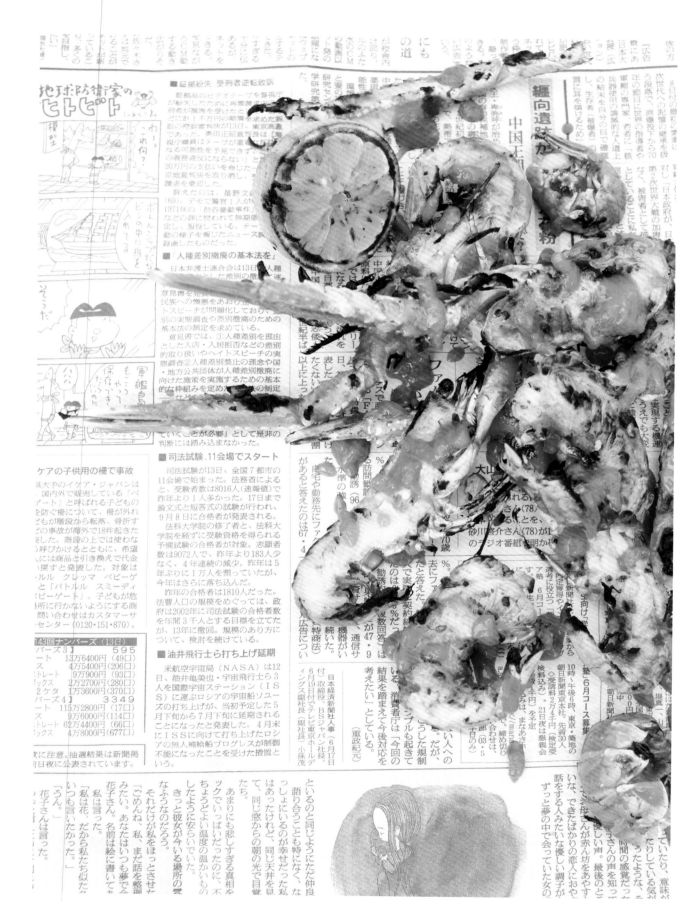

SUSHI'S FUCKED-UP FRIENDS

SUSHI

What does sushi mean to you? Is it something you have as a part of your selection at an Izakaya-type joint, a light lunch or snack? Or is sushi something worth making a pilgrimage for? Do you love and respect sushi creations as if they were something biblical?

When I was an apprentice chef, my chef took me to a sushi kitchen, you know the sushi-train joints? It was in Perth, Western Australia, and possibly one of the first sushi shops to hit town. It was called Jaws — hilarious name! Their strap line should have read 'If you can't beat 'em then eat 'em' (although eating them must count as beating them, right?). I don't recall this experience being mind-blowing in any way except for the playful name!

I continued to eat sushi from time to time, but it wasn't until I worked for Nobu that I began to understand how in-depth, how incredible and vast the world of sushi really was. People were living and breathing sushi, these guys were far more knowledgeable and respectful towards their craft than any other chef, baker or pastry chef I'd ever met. There was a seemingly good reason behind everything they did, including the excessive golf playing, gambling and whisky guzzling!

Their rice was warm; their fish cut just right so it was silky smooth; their seasonings and sauces were balanced so well. If you've ever considered yourself as a capable fishmonger of sorts (and before seeing these guys in action I did a little, I guess), go watch, or better still, work with a reputable team of sushi chefs. You'll feel like you're starting again, day one all over. You know nothing, grasshopper!

So I'd gone from seeing sushi as something of a mild fascination that I could take or leave. I didn't think much of cold take away sushi or even the stuff I'd tried to make myself, but now I was totally blown away.

I had never known what sushi was in the first place. All those shitty versions were like an out of work cover band and these guys were fucking Motorhead, tearing your head off on the main stage at the best music festival you've ever been to.

I can't say I'm very good at sushi, I've never focused on it, and if I had done I still might not have enough years under my belt to be as good as some of the guys I used to work with. However, I do have loads of respect for the basics of sushi and I'll always approach my sushi creations with a little caution.

Having said all that, I'm all about breaking the rules so whilst I always give a nod to certain rules and traditions I still think sushi fillings or toppings should be fucked with.

The sushi recipes in this chapter are the kind of recipes that sushi traditionalists would probably baulk at. They don't align with all the rules and they include ingredients that might be unwelcome to sushi purists. Maybe these creations are sushi's fucked up friends, but if sushi was a clean living, yoga-lovin' society, then these guys would be the punks in the beerlight, doing burnouts.

(Apologies David Berman, Silver Jews)

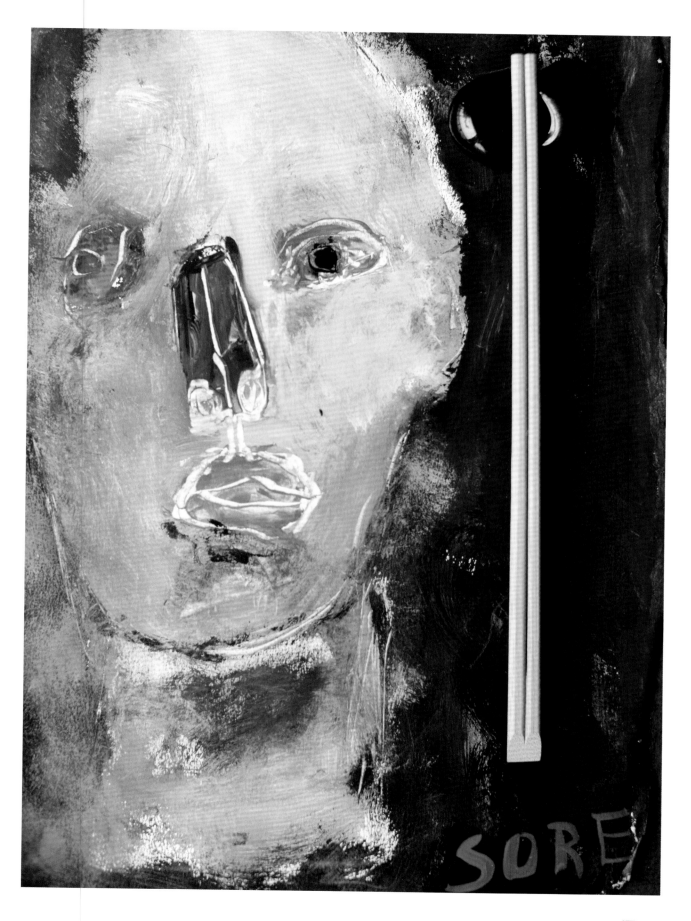

TEA-SMOKED SALMON GUNKAN AND YUZU KOSHO MAYO

This type of sushi is often referred to in Japan as 'gunkan', which means battleship. Now, a question for you, the reader: is this because:

a) it looks like a toy battleship, or
b) when they're too big, they're a fucking battle to get in your mouth?

(I'm pretty sure it's A)

Choose whichever answer you fancy most.

MAKES 5 GUNKAN

150g prepared sushi rice (see page 250)

5 strips nori, cut into 16cm × 3cm lengths

1 tablespoon yuzu kosho mayo (see page 251)

5 × 3cm strips takuan (daikon pickled with turmeric, available in Japanese shops. If you can't find it make your own version, or use the daikon amazu pickle – see page 248 but replace the cucumber with daikon – very different, but it works)

garlic crisps (see page 37)

For the hot-smoked salmon

30g sea salt, crushed until fine

¼ teaspoon sansho pepper

30g soft light brown sugar

3cm piece kombu, broken into tiny pieces and then pulverised in a mortar and pestle

a tiny pinch of shichimi togorashi

150g salmon belly (or the fattiest part you can find, ask a fishmonger for this, they might even give it to you for free!) (you need about 100g for this recipe, but start out with 150g as you'll need to test it a few times)

smoke mix (see page 104)

First, make the hot-smoked salmon. Mix together all the ingredients except the salmon and the smoke mix. Rub this mixture all over the salmon and pour over any excess mixture. Tightly wrap the salmon in clingfilm and refrigerate for 2 hours.

Rinse off the salt mix and leave to dry on kitchen paper.

Heat the smoke mix in a wok, or large pan, and get it smoking heavily – so heavy that it stains the walls yellow. Shake it around so that it's smoking evenly.

Place the cured salmon on a lightly oiled wire rack and drop this over the billowing smoke. Whack another wok or bowl that snuggly fits the diameter of the smoking wok on top to seal. Keep the heat on high.

Apart from adding a smoky taste, hot smoking is also about cooking the produce, too. For a 150g piece of salmon, you'll need to leave it for a good 5 minutes.

Remove the salmon from the wok and let it cool down completely. Then wrap in clingfilm and refrigerate for at least 8 hours. Initially, salmon hot-smoked this way tastes like the first time you drank used engine oil – the first cup actually makes you suck your gums back (apologies Ade Edmonson)! Chilling it allows the astringencies to die down and the overall taste is far more pleasant.

When you're ready to use it, break the hot-smoked salmon into small chunks.

Let's build a battleship!

Portion your prepared sushi rice into about 30g balls and mould these into oval shapes, about 1–1.5cm tall. Wrap the nori strips around the rice, creating the hulls of the ship (see the picture opposite). Now it's time to fill 'er up, sailor.

Poke a generous amount of broken up smoked salmon into the hull. Add a couple of generous squirts of the yuzu kosho mayo, one starboard, one port side of your battleship (newbies, these are not cooking terms but nautical terms – don't go asking fellow foodies if they dress their sea bass on the starboard side!).

Decorate with the takuan and the garlic crisps. Eat now. Don't let these hang around for too long after making them – the nori strips will go wrinkly like toes in the bath.

SPICY TUNA MAKI ROLL

First up, what's maki? Essentially it's rolled sushi, usually with nori (seaweed) and rice rolled around different fillings.

Too often I experience 'spicy tuna' in maki form or even tartare, etc., and it really isn't spicy at all. What's the point? Ok, let's not totally kill the flavour of the tuna unless you are attempting to use that bright pink, gas-infused shit that is looming in giant freezer warehouses worldwide. In which case it has no flavour anyway - go crazy with distracting accompaniments.

Generally, you're looking for a deeper red colour when purchasing tuna - this being its natural colour and most likely offering a better depth of flavour. If somebody tries selling you bright pink, almost translucent tuna beat them with it. (Not sure I can/should say that?)

So, this spicy tuna filling is spicy - it's not OTT spicy, but is good enough to get the title spicy without being too spicy for the tuna. If you like it spicier, don't add more of the sauce, spice it with some Blair's 3am Reserve Hot Sauce - that shit will kick your ass into next week. Be super-careful with it though; no matter how well you think you can handle chilli, this will take you down. We do a roulette maki with it in the restaurant; we cut the maki into six pieces and one of them gets a tiny dab of the 3am sauce - pain ensues.

MAKES 1 ROLL

100g prepared sushi rice (see page 250)

1 sheet nori, about 15 x 9cm

35–50ml spicy Korean miso (see page 249), plus extra for drizzling

120g best-quality yellow fin tuna, sinew removed and cut into approx. 1mm dice (blue fin is fine too, so long as it's from sustainable stock)

tempura crunchies (see page 50, quadruple the quantity of batter to give you enough for the maki)

To serve

2 lengths spring onion, green and white part, finely sliced, washed and dried

black and white sesame seeds

a few chives, chopped

Blair's 3am Reserve Hot Sauce, optional

Equipment

sushi mat

This is an uramaki-style roll which means it's inside out. Whenever you make an inside out roll, you need to tightly wrap your sushi mat in clingfilm. Here's a sweet tip for you: to make sure the clingfilm stays in place, grab your hairdryer and, once wrapped, give the clingfilm a full-on blast on a high setting. This will stick the clingfilm to the sushi mat.

Once you've wrapped your sushi mat in clingfilm you're ready to go. Using wet fingers, press your sushi rice into the nori sheet, spreading it evenly and leaving a 1cm border at the top edge. Flip the sheet over so that the nori faces upwards and the rice is touching your clingfilm.

Mix the spicy Korean miso, to taste, with the diced tuna. Make a thick line of it along the nori, about 1.5cm away from the edge closest to you. Lift the edge over the tuna mix and start to form a roll. Press firmly with the mat and try to use your fingers to press it evenly and manipulate it into a square shape.

Once it's square-ish, press all 4 sides of the maki roll so that it is firm and not in danger of falling apart when you go to slice it.

Make the tempura crunchies as instructed on page 50. (Depending on the size of your crunchies you might need to break them up a bit so they're not too big.) Roll the maki in the crunchies, make sure you apply pressure and cover all parts of the maki.

Slice the maki, using a lightly dampened blade, into 6 pieces. To serve up, drizzle with some extra spicy Korean miso, a scattering of spring onions, black and white sesame seeds, chopped chives, and, if you want to test how many schouilles of chilli you can handle, a tiny dot of Blair's 3am Sauce on 1 or more of the pieces.

SALMON GRAVADLAX MAKI IN DILL MAYO

Gravadlax – yep, the Swedish classic. But this is sushi you say? No, I tell you, this is one of sushi's fucked up friends. Purists will tell you how this offends them, how it breaks their arbitrary rules and that it instigates heated discussions amongst hard-working sushi chefs who spend their days otherwise playing golf, spinning their wheels and churning out perfectly honed mounds of glum – just like their grey personalities. Tradition has a place of course, but we shouldn't get hung up on it. Gravadlax is a tradition too, and in my opinion is an obvious preparation for sushi, err, sorry, maki.

This is a favourite of mine, see what you think...

MAKES 1 ROLL

80g gravadlax salmon cure (see below)

100g salmon fillet, skinless and boneless

a large bunch of dill, roughly chopped, plus extra to decorate

1 sheet nori, about 15cm x 9cm

100g prepared sushi rice (see page 250)

15g cucumber batons, deseeded, or avocado wedges

20g yuzu kosho mayo (see page 251), mixed with a large pinch of chopped dill

puffed soba (see page 248)

For the gravadlax salmon cure

50g fine sea salt

50g caster sugar

a decent pinch of ground white pepper

a decent pinch of shichimi togarashi

finely grated zest of ½ lemon

1 medium-sized beetroot, grated (this is messy shit – wear gloves, rubber ones, not your aunt's white cotton driving gloves)

Equipment

sushi mat

To make the gravadlax salmon, blend all the ingredients for the cure until fine and keep refrigerated until required.

Lay out a double layer of clingfilm – it needs to be big enough to accommodate your slab of salmon and be able to wrap it up as well. Spread a large dollop of the cure mix onto the clingfilm, place the salmon on top and rub the remaining cure mix over the top of the salmon. Fold the clingfilm up and around the salmon so that it is as tightly wrapped as possible; wrap some more clingfilm around it if necessary. Get it into the fridge for 1 hour to marinate. (You might need to give it longer, another hour or so, if you have a very large chunk of salmon from the head end of the fish.)

When the time is up, unwrap and wipe off the marinade. Lightly rinse under cold water and dry very well using kitchen paper. Grab the chopped dill, and then roll the salmon in it. Wrap once again in clingfilm and refrigerate for at least 30 minutes before using. This keeps well for a day; it's possible to keep longer, but it's not going to be at its best.

Wrap your sushi mat in clingfilm (see page 134 for my top tip).

Have ready a small bowl of cold water to keep your hands moist and the rice from sticking. Put the nori sheet on top of your sushi mat. Now you need to spin your nori sheet around from how you normally roll a maki so that it's more portrait than landscape.

Using wet fingers, press your sushi rice firmly into the nori sheet, spreading it evenly and leaving a 1cm border at the top edge. Flip the rice sheet over so that the maki faces upwards and the rice is touching your sushi mat. Before cutting your strips of gravadlax to go in the centre of the maki, cut some thin slices across the face of the fillet so that it looks like thin strips of sashimi – set these to one side and use the rest of the salmon to fill the maki, along with the cucumber or avocado. Starting from the bottom end (the end closest to you), and, using both hands, start rolling the nori sheet tightly ensuring that the fillings don't pop out the sides and that they remain central once you reach the 1cm nori lip. With the sushi mat on the outside of the maki, use small amounts of even pressure to ensure all parts of the maki are nice and tight. Unravel the maki from the mat, and layer the reserved slices of the gravadlax over your maki roll, so that they overlap. Cut into 6 pieces.

Top each piece with a small dollop of the mayo, some puffed soba and some chopped dill. (Don't serve soy sauce with this, it's flavoursome enough and has its own sauce already.)

SOFT-SHELL CRAB TEMPURA MAKI WITH KIMCHI

There must be hundreds of different versions of this maki worldwide. I always order a soft-shell maki if I see it on a menu, I'm a kind of fan. Sometimes these rolls are described as spider rolls: WTF? Something about that name pisses me off. I'm not exactly sure what it is about it that is such a wind-up. I'll have somebody assess my brain one day and the truth will be known – it might be such a dull reason that it's just not worth repeating or even tweeting. I suppose this name isn't so bad compared to what should be crowned as the world's most ridiculously named sushi – the 'fashion sandwich' from South Africa. Can you imagine coming up with that name and then having the balls to tell somebody that you're going to unleash a new dish called the fashion sandwich? Unless it was a comedian I can't see how it could be taken seriously – a prank gone wrong perhaps? Surely it has nothing to do with fashion in the original sense of the word. Anyway, back to my soft-shell crab roll, without the silly title.

MAKES 1 ROLL

45g soft-shell crab (about ½ crab, cooked weight)
1 litre rapeseed oil, for deep-frying
20g tempura flour, for coating
200ml trisol batter (see page 251)
1 sheet nori, about 15cm x 9cm

For the maki filling
100g prepared sushi rice (see page 250)
15g kimchi mayo (see page 246)
6 cucumber batons, deseeded
3 avocado wedges

To serve
25g kimchi pickle (see page 246)
kimchi mayo (see page 246)
1 tablespoon chopped chives

Equipment
sushi mat

First, make sure your crab is well drained. Wrap it in multiple layers of kitchen paper and gently press any excess water out of it.

Heat the oil in a fryer or large pan to 180°C/350°F. Toss the crab in tempura flour to lightly coat then drop into the hot oil and fry for 4 minutes. Be careful as this will create small explosions and spit hot oil at you. Remove the tempura crab from the oil, using a perforated spoon, drain on a wire rack and cool to room temperature.

Keep your oil at 180°C/350°F. Cut the just-fried crab into 6 even pieces, then dip each piece into the trisol batter and fry again, this time for about 1½ minutes. You will now have some seriously moisty-moist yet damn crunchy crab. Remove, set it aside and you're ready to roll in to your maki.

Wrap your sushi mat in clingfilm (see page 134 for my top tip). Gather all of your maki filling ingredients, plus a small bowl of cold water to keep your hands moist and the rice from sticking to them. Put the nori sheet on top of your clingfilm-wrapped sushi mat. Now you need to spin your nori sheet around from how you normally roll a maki so that it's more portrait than landscape.

Using wet fingers, press your sushi rice firmly into the nori sheet, spreading it evenly and leaving a 1cm border at the top edge. Flip the rice sheet over so that the nori faces upwards and the rice is touching your sushi mat. Spread or squirt over a small line of kimchi mayo. Top as evenly as possible with the cucumber, avocado and crunchy crab. To close up, start from the bottom end (the end closest to you), and, using both hands, start rolling the maki tightly ensuring that the fillings don't pop out the sides and that they remain central once you reach the 1cm nori lip. With the sushi mat on the outside of the maki, use small amounts of even pressure to ensure all parts of the maki are nice and tight. Unravel the maki from the mat and cut into 6 pieces.

Serve up with some kimchi on the side and a drizzle of kimchi mayo and some chopped chives over the top.

Arrrrrrgh
Joe's at it
again

SCORCHED WAGYU ROLL TOPPED WITH CHICKEN LIVER PARFAIT AND YUZU MARMALADE

Purists and snobs of both French and Japanese cuisines would probably crap themselves at the thought of hooking these two dishes together. The initial idea is a total rip-off of Tournedos Rossini – a classic French steak and foie gras dish. Rossini was a well-known eighteenth-century Italian composer who was mates with French culinary master Marie-Antoine Carême. Some say that Carême came up with this for Rossini and simply named it after him. Another version suggests that Rossini came up with it himself after his foie gras appetiser and main course steak showed up at the table at the same time, and he simply slid one on top of the other.

There's no foie gras in this recipe – I've switched it up for a very creamy chicken liver parfait. Stupidly extravagant and way over the top, I'd like to crown this roll the heavyweight champion of the nouveau-riche sushi – worldwide!

The marmalade makes more than needed for the recipe so serve leftovers with sautéed lobster and chillies with some lemon, or it's great with vanilla ice cream.

MAKES 6 PIECES

60g Wagyu slider mix (see page 67, and scale down quantities as necessary)
light olive oil, for frying
1 spring onion, sliced into thin rounds, washed in cold water and drained
sesame seeds, to serve
sea salt and freshly ground black pepper

For the yuzu marmalade

100g grated yuzu zest (frozen or fresh)
90ml fresh lemon juice
40ml orange juice
40g caster sugar
3g powdered pectin, mixed with a little lukewarm water to form a paste
1 teaspoon yuzu juice
1 teaspoon liquid glucose, optional

For the chicken liver parfait

300ml port
2 cloves garlic, crushed
50g shallots, peeled and thinly sliced
300g chicken livers, trimmed of sinew, rinsed and drained
2 eggs
300g salted butter, melted and clarified, plus extra to top
a pinch of sea salt and ground white pepper

ingredients continued on page 142

The marmalade, chicken liver parfait and burgers could easily be made a day or so ahead if you want to be prepared.

Make the yuzu marmalade by mixing the ingredients, except the yuzu juice and glucose, in a pan. Heat until lightly bubbling but don't let it boil. Remove from the heat and leave to cool to room temperature, then stir through the yuzu juice. Taste – if you find it is too sharp, add the liquid glucose. The marmalade keeps well in the fridge for 1 month in a sterilised jar, but serve it at room temperature.

To make the chicken liver parfait, combine the port, garlic and shallots and simmer over a medium heat until reduced by two-thirds. Strain and then allow to cool to room temperature, which should take about 20 minutes.

Preheat the oven to around 110°C/90°C fan/Gas Mark ¼.

Blend the chicken livers on a high speed for 1 minute in a blender, slowly add the eggs, then trickle in the port reduction and season with sea salt and white pepper.

With the motor still running on a steady speed, slowly pour the warm clarified butter into the liver mixture so that it emulsifies.

Pour the chicken liver mixture into a small terrine mould or individual ramekins, and put the mould or ramekins in a roasting tray. Pour hot water into the roasting tray, using enough to come at least halfway up the sides of the moulds or ramekins. Bake in the oven in your water bath for 1½ hours.

Remove the parfait from the oven and allow to cool for 1 hour. Once it's at room temperature, pour over a thin layer of lukewarm clarified butter and then chilli in the fridge for 2 or 3 hours before use. (This recipe will make more than you need, but the layer of clarified butter will help preserve the parfait in the fridge for a week or so.)

recipe continued on page 142

For the sushi roll

20g cucumber batons

30ml amazu, chilled (see page 248)

1 sheet nori

100g prepared sushi rice (see page 250),
   at room temperature

5g wasabi paste (fresh is best,
   rehydrated, good-quality powdered
   is quite suitable but the cheap, bright
   green tube-stuff is total crap)

**For the yuzu marmalade-miso
sauce**

50ml den miso (see page 244)

1 tablespoon rice vinegar

½ teaspoon Japanese mustard powder,
   mixed with a little water to form
   a wet paste

2 tablespoons yuzu marmalade (see
   page 141)

Equipment

sushi mat

Soak the cucumber batons in the cold amazu for 1 hour. Set aside.

Next, combine the ingredients for the Wagyu mini-burgers according to the recipe on page 67. Then, with clean hands, divide the mix into six 10g piles. Lightly moisten your hands and shape each pile into mini-burger shapes. Cover with clingfilm and refrigerate for at least 20 minutes prior to cooking. You are ready to roll…

Heat a non-stick frying pan, season your mini Wagyu sliders/burgers with a little sea salt and freshly ground black pepper. Add a splash of olive oil to the pan, and fry the burgers over a high heat for about 1½ minutes on each side. The result should see a well-browned exterior with a pink centre. Keep warm.

Next maki the maki roll. Wrap your sushi mat in clingfilm (see page 134 for my top tip), gather your nori sheet, sushi rice and wasabi, and drain your pickled cucumber batons.

Place the nori sheet onto the plastic wrapped sushi mat. Lightly dampen your hands – rub together with a little water so that you have a light, even coating of water all over your hands/fingers – and then press the sushi rice evenly over the entire sheet of nori, leaving a gap of about 8mm at the top end (furthest from you). Flip it over so that the nori is facing upwards.

Drain off any excess pickling liquid from the cucumbers by letting them sit on some kitchen paper for 1 minute, then place them evenly in the centre of the nori. Take the wasabi with your index finger and do a long, even as possible, swoosh along the exposed nori nearest to you, below the cucumber. Roll it up, press the roll firmly whilst inside the mat to ensure everything is sticking and it won't fall apart. Cut into 6 pieces.

Quickly mix together the ingredients for the marmalade-miso sauce.

Top each maki piece with a burger, a small teaspoon of the chicken liver parfait, a pinch of spring onion, a scattering of sesame seeds and some random splashings of the yuzu marmalade-miso sauce. (You could just serve the sauce in a dipping cup on the side if you're not feeling too artistic.)

FRIED CHICKEN MAKI WITH UMAMI MAYO AND CHILLI PONZU

So I was working in Dubai, setting up this posh Japanese joint and our manager, no, hold on, 'director' (who was fresh out of Make-a-Manager School) had a thing for fried food with a triple side of mayo. As a total piss-take I made him a fried chicken maki, he loved it and didn't see my sarcastic maki as a piss-take, but wanted more. Animal, I thought. This didn't satisfy me so I had to do one worse. A day or so later it was lasagne for the staff meal – yep, lasagne maki. He was dubious, but, like a hesitant stray cat he drew himself closer, sniffed, then went for the kill! I gave up after that, I figured this guy would eat anything around and I couldn't think of anything more fucked up than lasagne in a maki.

Anyway, the chicken maki turned out to be pretty decent. Here's a version…

MAKES 1 ROLL

1 sheet nori
2 pieces fried chicken (see page 71), cut into strips
100g prepared sushi rice (see page 250)
2 teaspoons umami mayo (see page 67), plus extra to serve

For the chilli ponzu dipping sauce

1 red chilli, roughly chopped (choose something scorching hot)
80ml ponzu sauce (see page 247)
1 teaspoon lime juice
a pinch of chopped spring onion

To serve

1 tablespoon chopped, washed and dried spring onion
6 thin slices red chilli

Equipment

sushi mat

First make the chilli ponzu dipping sauce. Mix all the ingredients together and steep at room temperature for 1 day. Refrigerate until required.

To make the maki, lay the nori sheet onto a sushi mat layered with a sheet of clingfilm. With damp hands, press the prepared sushi rice onto the nori and spread it evenly across the top of the sheet. Flip it over so the nori is now facing up.

Lay 1cm-thick strips of the fried chicken along the top of the nori sheet, leaving a gap of about 1.5cm from the edge closest to you. Squirt a thin stream of umami mayo next to the chicken.

Roll up the nori and press firmly to ensure all is being held in place.

With a damp, thin blade, cut the maki into 6 even pieces and serve up. Drizzle over some more umami mayo, decorate with the spring onion and chilli, and serve with the chilli ponzu on the side as a dip.

CHIVE OMELETTE NIGIRI TOPPED WITH FRESH TRUFFLE SHAVINGS

Tamago-yaki can be pretty special if done well. But it takes a fair bit of practice and unless you're being served by a master of it, you may just be eating two-day-old cold egg omelette. One of the best versions, in my opinion, is made with pounded shrimp and it's fairly sweet. Traditionally, the egg mixture would be cooked in layers using a square copper pan. It would be added a ladleful at a time, allowed to cook and then rolled up to the back of the pan, then the next ladle would go in until you had a full pan of cooked tamago-yaki. It takes ages and this method is not only quicker but you can do it in much smaller quantities. Fresh is best, yo.

MAKES 5 NIGIRI

For the omelette

50g peeled and deveined tiger prawns
2 eggs (really fucking good ones, make
   an effort), whisked
30ml dashi (see page 245)
15ml mirin
½ tablespoon light soy sauce
a pinch of flaked sea salt
10g caster sugar
1 tablespoon chopped chives
a few drops of white truffle oil
grapeseed oil, for greasing

For the nigiri

150g prepared sushi rice (see page 250)
1 sheet nori, cut into 5 × 6–7cm strips
10g truffle shavings, fresh only or
don't bother

Pound or blend the prawns until you have a tight purée. Whisk the eggs with all the other ingredients except the oil, and mix in the prawn purée. Cover with clingfilm and refrigerate for a minimum of 1 hour or a maximum of overnight. This allows the air bubbles to disappear and the prawn flavour to develop.

So, time to cook.

The best scenario is to use a really wide frying pan. Set it over a medium heat and lightly oil it with some grapeseed oil. Move the oil around the pan, then, using kitchen paper, wipe the pan – it shouldn't be totally dry, but there should just be a thin layer of oil.

Pour in a layer of the egg and allow it to set, which should happen almost immediately. Remove from the heat and, using an angled spatula, roll up the omelette into a cigar shape and slide it out of the pan onto a plate to cool. (If you have extra egg left over make another omelette.) Refrigerate the omelettes for 35 minutes or so.

Once cooled, cut the omelette on an acute angle so that you get an 8cm or so long slice.

Divide the sushi rice into 5 and, with damp hands, shape the balls into rectangles. Lay each omelette slice over a rice pillow and with dampened hands gently press the omelette onto the rice.

Strap the omelette to the rice using a strip of nori, shave over some fresh truffle and serve.

MISO GRILLED FOIE GRAS NIGIRI WITH GREEN APPLE OROSHI

Foie gras - touchy subject to some and that's fair enough. Some foie gras birds do get reared poorly but so do chickens and pigs and so on. I think it's a matter of sourcing the most ethically treated, well-reared meats that you can.

I've visited foie gras farmers in France who care for their birds, which are free-range and live in the most incredible pristine hills. I wrote a book about foie gras once, talk about niche! I've eaten some fantastic foie gras over the years but this method for pan-frying it destroys them all. It adds a shit-ton of umami,

and an element of sugar and mirin which helps the foie gras to caramelise beautifully.

So, on to the miso part. Marinating things in miso sauce can be seriously brilliant. The famous Japanese black cod dish is simply black cod in miso sauce and soaked for three days. However, not everything works in my opinion. Salmon, for example, doesn't have enough fat unless you're using the belly, and then it is insanely good. Foie gras is pretty much all fat, so miso sauce won't be drying it out too easily.

Miso and foie gras 4eva!

MAKES 5 NIGIRI

100g slice of foie gras, approx. 1–1.5cm thick

30–40ml den miso, or just enough to cover (see page 244)

150g prepared sushi rice (see page 250)

drizzle olive oil

1 sheet nori, cut into 5 x6cm-long strips

sea salt and freshly ground black pepper

To serve

2 teaspoons unagi sauce (see page 251)

puffed soba (see page 248)

½ Granny Smith apple

5 slices cucumber, cut on an angle if you're fancy

Combine the foie gras with the den miso and refrigerate, covered, for 18–24 hours.

When you're ready to begin making your sushi, divide the rice into 5 equal-sized balls and then shape into rectangular blocks.

Heat a heavy non-stick pan until almost smoking and then drip in a tiny amount of olive oil in and tilt the pan to spread the oil around.

Season the foie gras lightly with some sea salt and freshly ground black pepper on both sides (I fucking hate chefs who are too lazy to season anything on both sides). Pan-fry the foie gras on one side for approximately 1 minute, until well caramelised. Flip it over and cook the other side for 45 seconds–1 minute. You need the colouring process to happen fast – the foie gras will burn if it sits there for too long and cooking it at a lower temperature will overcook it.

Remove the foie gras and rest on a warm plate in a warm place for 2 minutes – it should be soft and molten inside, perfect.

Slice it on an angle and place each slice over a block of the shaped rice. Strap it in place using a strip of nori.

Drizzle with some unagi sauce, top with some puffed soba and freshly grated apple (you want to grate the apple just before you're going to use it or it will discolour). Serve on some cucumber slices and consume it quickly.

DASHI POACHED VEAL NIGIRI WITH ANCHOVY MAYO

This is a version of the fantastic Piedmontese dish, *vitello tonnato*. I've come across a few different variations for what is essentially roasted or braised veal with a kind of tuna mayo. It can be dressed with capers, anchovies and cayenne pepper too, and that's what I've done here. I leave the veal fillet to slowly poach in lots of dashi, away from direct heat, then chill, slice and shape the nigiri. The must-have toppings are fried capers and anchovy mayo.

Certainly it's a massive shift from the norm when it comes to nigiri but if it works, then who gives a shit really. I used to take a far more traditional or 'correct' stance myself, but how could anything ever develop if we all thought this way?

You're better off cooking more veal than you need, and it needs to be the weight suggested below so that overcooking doesn't occur, but we all love to eat the trimmings – lots of trimmings.

MAKES 5 NIGIRI

200g veal fillet
1 litre dashi (see page 245)
5cm piece kombu
100ml light soy sauce
5 salted capers
rapeseed oil, for deep-frying
150g prepared sushi rice (see page 250)
black and white sesame seeds, to serve

For the anchovy mayo
100g mayonnaise
35g anchovies in olive oil
3 teaspoons lemon juice
1 teaspoon yuzu juice
2 garlic cloves, finely chopped

Cut the veal fillet lengthways in half then estimate your 200g rectangular 'log' and portion it off.

Heat the dashi, kombu and light soy sauce in a saucepan to come up to 90°C/195°F, and maintain this temperature for 5 minutes.

Remove from the heat and allow the temperature to drop to 75°C/170°F, then drop in your 200g veal 'log'. Keep your pan off the heat. Set a timer for 20 minutes then remove the veal. Take a slice off one end – it ought to be rose pink. Return the veal into the dashi-soy mixture to cool for 30–40 minutes until completely cold, then refrigerate.

While the veal is chilling, make the anchovy mayo by blending all the ingredients until super-fine. Chill until required.

When the veal is chilled, slice it on an angle so that you have five 6cm-long slices.

Rinse the capers to remove the salt and then pat them completely dry. Heat the oil in a fryer or large pan to 180°C/350°F. Deep-fry for 1 minute, until crunchy. Remove with a perforated scoop and drain on kitchen paper. Store in a warm dry place until you need them.

Divide the sushi rice into 5 balls and, with damp hands, shape them into rectangular pillows.

One by one, lay a slice of veal over each the rice pillow. With freshly dampened hands, press the veal slice onto the rice whilst holding the base in your other hand. Now shape it to fit over the sides, so that it looks nice and neat and rounded at the sides. Repeat with the other 4 nigiri.

Top with a small dollop of the anchovy mayo, some sesame seeds and a fried caper. No extra soy sauce on the side is necessary with this, but a little extra anchovy mayo never hurts…

CRUNCHY TEMAKI CONES

Temaki is the variety of sushi which gets wrapped up like an ice cream cone. Essentially, these cones get dehydrated with mirin so they become extra crunchy and remain crunchier a little longer. It's a pretty sweet idea and it hails from my mate Maru, a fellow Japanese chef here in London. I've made mini cones here but you could just as easily do larger ones, just dry them out for a little longer.

Fill these with whatever you like - spicy tuna tartar, chunky avocado, gravadlax, salmon and dill mayo or fried soft shell crab, or have a go at the king crab in yuzu kosho mayo as below. They're best eaten immediately after filling so that the nori still has a bit of crunch and hasn't become soggy and a little chewy.

MAKES 6 MINI CONES (YOU MIGHT HAVE A BIT OF FILLING LEFT OVER)

3 sheets nori, cut in half diagonally
    to make 6 triangles in total
15ml mirin, for brushing

For the king crab filling

60g cooked king crab, cut into chunks
    (no worries if you don't have king crab –
    chose your preferred crab instead)
25g yuzu kosho mayo (see page 252)
1 teaspoon lime juice
2 teaspoons chopped chives
2 teaspoons finely chopped red onion
a tiny pinch of sea salt
1–2 grinds of freshly ground black pepper

Equipment

6 metal pastry cones – try to find Teflon
    ones or wrap your aluminium ones
    in parchment paper first

Brush the nori sheets liberally with mirin, then shape each wet nori sheet around a cone to fashion a nori-shaped cone. Place these in a dehydrator overnight for a good 8–12 hours, until they are properly crunchy. No dehydrator? Try doing this in your oven at it's lowest setting (around 70°C/50°C fan/Gas Mark very low) for 5–6 hours.

Store the cones in an airtight container. Tip: purchase some silica gel online and pour a layer of this into the bottom of your container. Place a sheet of parchment over the top of this, then store your cones on top of the parchment – the gel will eat up the moisture and leave your cones super-crunchy.

When you're nearly ready to serve, mix together the crab filling ingredients and fill your cones with a little almost overflowing. Serve right away and enjoy the crunch.

CHIRASHI SUSHI BITES

Chirashi sushi is, simply put, various ingredients - usually sashimi, ikura (salmon roe) or omelette - served on top of slightly warm, seasoned sushi rice. It's one of the true joys I've come across at Tskuji, Tokyo's famous fish market. Rock up at 4am and get ready for a breakfast like no other, large beer and some mind-blowing, yet-to-be refrigerated fish on warm, ultra-fresh sushi rice. I've never had fish so flavoursome, so fresh, so firm yet creamy. This was one of the most incredible food experiences for me ever! All self-proclaimed foodies - you haven't tasted the real deal until you've been to Tskuji, make it your next holiday; you'll not be disappointed and you'll most certainly be humbled.

Although this is one hell of a dish, it wouldn't work on a Kurobuta menu. We serve smaller dishes, tapas style, and a bowl of chirashi is almost a meal in itself. We started to play around with a mini version of chirashi in another restaurant I worked in. Our talented head sushi chef, Maru, came up with a killer version, which we called 'chirashi bites'. This is a version of that. Want to do a sushi-based snack or dish to impress your friends but can't be arsed messing about with sushi or always fuck it up? Then this is for you.

Note that the below is just a basic topping, but you could go apeshit and add: sushi omelette, crispy leeks, sea bass sashimi, spring onion, blindingly ripe and eye-wateringly tasty cherry tomatoes, sesame seeds, sea urchin and scallops. The list goes on...

MAKE AS MANY AS YOU LIKE, PER PIECE YOU'LL NEED THE FOLLOWING:

1 baby gem lettuce leaf
½ heaped tablespoon freshly made, still
  warm sushi rice (see page 250)

For the topping

1 x 7g slice salmon sashimi
1 x 7g slice tuna sashimi
½ teaspoon ikura (salmon roe) (insider's
  tip – marinate briefly in a 1:1 solution
  of soy sauce and mirin)
1 x 7g slice yellowtail sashimi
½ small leek, cut into thin strips and
  quickly fried

For the nikiri shoyu (this is what I serve if somebody asks for soy), to serve

4 parts dark soy sauce
1 part sake
1 part mirin

Mix the nikiri shoyu together according to how much you want to make. Next, simply put the warm rice on the baby gem leaf, add the toppings, and drizzle with the nikiri shoyu. Serve immediately, whilst it's still warm, or this won't be anywhere near as nice as it should be.

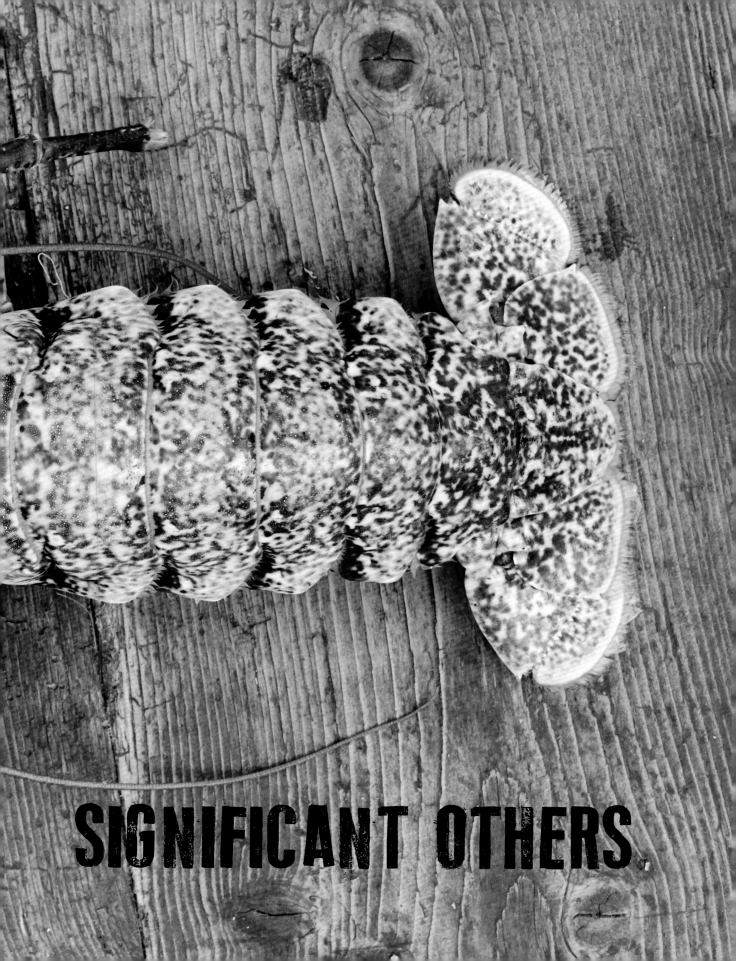

SIGNIFICANT OTHERS

PAN-FRIED DUCK ROLL

Essentially this is a kind of 'pulled' duck confit, rolled up, sliced and pan-fried. Jeez, I'm so over the term 'pulled'. In this instance, it's a good way to describe what happens during the preparation process, but on the flip side, I'm now in danger of attracting hipsters, you know, those creative beardy types who can only eat local butter from a one-cow dairy, make eldercurrant drinks from their own piss and of course almost choke to death when they find out their 'aged jus burger' hasn't been made from 'pulled meat' – back to your cycle cafés to sip your cold brew!

Back to the duck rolls... let's say that the flesh of our confit is 'shredded'; let's get in fast with this one, before our hippy-hipster mates turn that into an annoying word too.

SERVES 2, AS PART OF A MULTI-COURSE MENU

2 duck legs
½ recipe bacon cure (see page 111)
2 litres duck fat
5cm piece kombu
3cm piece ginger, sliced
a few generous shakes of sansho pepper
potato starch, for dusting
grapeseed oil, for frying
a handful of unsalted cashew nuts, deep-fried untill golden, to garnish
ponzu sauce (see page 247), to serve, optional
sea salt and freshly ground black pepper

Rub the bacon cure into the duck legs, making sure you rub it all over. Cover and refrigerate for 12 hours. Rinse off the cure and pat the legs dry with kitchen paper.

Heat the duck fat in an ovenproof pan to 85°C and preheat your oven to this temperature too (85°C/65°C fan/Gas Mark low). Add the kombu and ginger slices to the pan and when the oil reaches temperature, carefully put in the cured duck legs and cover with foil. Cook in the oven for 12 hours. (You could also use a sous vide machine, should you have one.)

After 12 hours, remove the pan from the oven and allow the duck legs to cool in the fat.

Slip on some rubber food prep gloves and lift the confit legs from the fat. Shred – don't pull – the meat away from the bones, discarding all the bones and mysterious tough bits. Shred the meat fibres as finely as you think you can, and season with the sansho pepper and a pinch of salt and black pepper. Drop 4–5 tablespoons of the duck fat into the shredded meat and mix thoroughly.

Lay out some clingfilm on the worktop and divide the meat into 3 even sausage-like shapes, then wrap them, one by one, as tightly as you can, still in the sausage shapes, about 2½–3cm round. Tie each end of the clingfilm. I'm putting emphasis on keeping it tight here – tight, tight, tight.

Get your 3 duck rolls in the fridge and chill for a good 5–6 hours.

Whilst still in clingfilm, cut the rolls into 5 slices, or if you fancy them a little smaller go for 6 per roll. Remove the clingfilm from each slice and dust the slices in potato starch.

Next, heat a decent puddle of grapeseed oil in the pan. Add the duck roll slices, and fry over a medium-high heat for 2 minutes on each side, until mildly crunchy.

Arrange the duck roll slices on your serving plate, garnish with some crushed fried cashews and serve with some ponzu sauce on the side if you like. You're ready to rock and roll, oooh yeah!

BUTA NO KAKUNI WITH JAPANESE MUSTARD

This bad boy is a classic Japanese nimono dish. Nimomo is one of the many categories of Japanese cooking and takes in all simmered dishes. This particular dish comes from Nagasaki, apparently one of the only ports open to foreign trade for 250 years. It is also one of the first places that meat dishes began to appear after Buddhism forbade the slaughter of four-legged animals.

I've seen various different versions of this dish. The common theme of course is the pork - it's always cooked very slowly and is, most of the time, really soft. And it's always served with mustard. The most interesting version I encountered came with a kind of congee (rice porridge). I'm a massive fan of congee so I fell for it immediately. Another version I've seen, actually this time in a Japanese cookery magazine, presented it with a soft-boiled egg. I can't really eat the egg due to hating raw yolks, but jeez, it looked pretty awesome. Here I've cooked both versions. It's all so soft and silky, so rich and so moreish. If I get to the stage where all my teeth fall out and I have to be fed soft goo, then I'd pray it was this, maybe minus the egg. Presumably I'd still be able to talk so I should be okay...

SERVES 6

600g pork belly, cut into 2cm-thick strips

For the pork marinade
800ml dashi (see page 245)
250ml sake
50ml mirin
100ml dark soy sauce
80g soft light brown sugar
8cm piece kombu

For the congee
200g sushi rice, unwashed
6cm piece kombu
4cm knob of ginger, sliced
6 grilled/roasted chicken wings
5 teaspoons light soy sauce
2 teaspoons roasted sesame oil
a large pinch of sea salt, to season
a pinch of ground white pepper,
    to season

For the soft eggs
6 eggs

To serve
a handful of chopped spring onions
S&B Japanese mustard, or rehydrate
    English mustard powder with a
    little water

Preheat the oven to 110°C/90°C fan/Gas Mark ¼.

Mix all the ingredients for the pork marinade together until the sugar dissolves. Next, place the pork in a large flameproof casserole, and pour over the marinade. Cover with a lid or foil, and set in the oven to cook for 7 hours – it's a long time but well worth it. Remove the casserole from the oven and allow the pork to cool in its liquid.

To make the congee, simmer the rice, 2 litres of water, kombu, ginger and chicken wings for 45 minutes to 1 hour (the timing will depend on how old the rice is), until soft and porridge-like. The congee will require continuous stirring and may need topping up with more water to prevent over-thickening.

To make the soft eggs, bring a pan of water to 63°C/145°F (use a thermometer), and carefully drop in your eggs. Cook for 45 minutes at a steady temperature and you'll have a perfectly cooked, runny yolk. If the temperature is creeping higher than the magic 63°C/145°F, throw in a couple of ice cubes. The beauty of this method is that you won't need to peel the egg – just give it a tap and pull the shell apart, your perfect egg will gently drop out.

Use a perforated spoon to remove the kombu, ginger and chicken wings from the congee. Season with the soy sauce, sesame oil, salt and pepper.

To serve, plate up 2 lengths of pork per person, add a decent dollop of the congee and top with an egg. Finish off with some chopped spring onion and a little pork cooking liquid (warmed up) and of course a dollop of S&B Japanese mustard – you can't eat it without this!

Enjoy, piggies!

MARBOU DOFU

This little cracker hails from the Sichuan province of China. Just like dozens of other food and culture influences, marbou dofu (aka mapo doufu or mapo tofu) has made its way into Japanese cuisine. Essentially, this is a one-pot dish of pork or beef mince with tofu, which has a rich fermented bean paste flavour and a warming chilli buzz. I've tried two main versions in Japan: marbou dofu (with tofu) and marbou nasu (with aubergine). When I first started to mess about with a recipe that I could serve at Kurobuta I couldn't decide between the nasu and tofu versions, so I added both.

This really is a killer comfort food dish if served on steaming hot rice. I wasn't brought up on it, but it reminds me a bit of my mum's 'mince on toast'. I serve it in lettuce cups at Kurobuta so it's lighter.

SERVES 2 AS PART OF A MULTI-COURSE MENU

1 litre rapeseed oil, for deep-frying

1 large purple aubergine, peeled and cut into large-ish 2.5cm chunks

20g ginger, finely grated or chopped

20g garlic, finely grated or chopped

20g spring onion, chopped

100g minced pork, from the shoulder

10g tobanjan (chilli bean paste)

10g gochujang (fermented chilli paste)

20g red miso paste

5 teaspoons mirin

50ml Chinese rice wine

150ml chicken stock

1 tablespoon cornflour, mixed with 1 tablespoon water to make a paste

4 teaspoons roasted sesame oil

2 tablespoons Japanese black vinegar

150g crumbled medium-firm tofu

1 tablespoon soft brown sugar

To serve
iceberg lettuce cups, optional

steamy hot rice, optional

First, heat the oil in your fryer (or large pan) to 180°C/350°F. Add the aubergine chunks, in batches if necessary, and deep-fry until golden. Drain well and set aside.

Sauté the ginger, garlic and spring onion over a medium heat until light brown in colour. Add the pork and tobanjan and brown the mince until cooked through. Add the gochujang, red miso, mirin and rice wine and cook for 2 minutes. Add the chicken stock and golden fried aubergine, then bring to the boil. Quickly stir in the cornflour-water mix and stir well until thoroughly incorporated. Simmer for 1 minute.

Remove from the heat and stir in the sesame oil, black vinegar and tofu. Gently stir in the sugar.

Serve warm with ice-cold crunchy iceberg lettuce cups, or on steamy hot rice if you fancy.

SOBA RISOTTO WITH BARLEY MISO GRILLED SALMON BELLY

I'm calling this a risotto because I think it's the easiest way to describe how this dish takes shape. It's actually far wetter than your average risotto.

You'll no doubt be familiar with soba noodles, which are produced by first milling the grain soba-ko (buckwheat) to flour, which is then mixed with wheat flour, water and salt to make up a dough. The next few steps are really interesting: the dough is rolled out with what looks like a street fighter's weapon. Once it's shaped correctly yet another weapon of a tool is unleashed - a giant square-shaped knife. (You should look it up, this bad boy is seriously dangerous!) Don't mess with any angry soba chef. Anyhow, these soba grains,

before the soba noodle dudes wind up with them and mill them to flour, make an excellent risotto-like dish. I make this with mushrooms or whatever green veg is in season - asparagus, broad beans, peas, etc.

If you struggle in your search for moro miso (barley miso), then you can go for a classic shio-yaki version whereby the skin side of the salmon receives a liberal sprinkling of fine salt before it's grilled. Note, moro miso differs from your basic soybean miso, which is easy to source, but I wouldn't recommend using soybean miso as a substitute.

I use Japanese soba grains here but you can substitute them with European buckwheat grains - after all, soba is Japanese for buckwheat.

SERVES 2 AS PART OF MULTI-COURSE MENU

1 x 180g salmon belly, skin on, bones removed
50g moro miso (barley miso)
light olive oil, for brushing

For the risotto
90g soba grains (or buckwheat grains)
40g salted butter
2 garlic cloves, thinly sliced
30g mixed Japanese mushrooms –
    shimeji, shiitake, eryngii – thinly sliced
2 asparagus stalks, sliced into rounds, or
    30g freshly blanched peas, or whatever
    is peaking in season green-veg wise
50ml sake
50ml mirin
50ml dark soy sauce
120ml dashi (see page 245)
10g cornflour, mixed with 1–2 tablespoons
    cold water to form a paste

To serve
1 tablespoon chives, chopped, optional
a few drops of truffle oil, optional

Equipment
3 long (18cm) bamboo skewers, pre-
    soaked in cold water for 1 hour

First prepare the salmon. Rub the salmon with the miso and marinate for a good 6–8 hours.

Put the soba grains in a pan with cold water to cover and bring to the boil. Simmer for about 6–7 minutes until the grains are tender. Drain and set aside.

Melt 30g of the butter in a pan. Add the garlic and sauté until soft, uncovered, over a medium heat for 2–3 minutes. Add the mushrooms and asparagus (or other green veg) and sauté for 2–3 minutes, until soft. Add the sake, mirin, soy sauce and dashi, and then add the pre-cooked soba grains and bring to the boil. Whisk in the cornflour-water mix and simmer for about 45 seconds.

Keep the risotto warm while you grill the salmon.

Remove the salmon from the marinade and poke the soaked skewers into it at even intervals along the long side of the salmon. (Each end piece needs to angle to a central point so that you can hold it with one hand.)

Place a grill rack over really hot, glowing charcoal. Lightly oil the marinated salmon and then place it on the rack, skin-side down. Grill for 3–4 minutes or until the skin becomes crunchy. Flip it over and cook for a further 2–3 minutes.

Just before serving, stir the remaining 10g of butter into the risotto and, if using, finish with the chives and/or a few drops of truffle oil. To serve, spoon the soba risotto into a bowl and place the salmon right on top.

Go for gold!

BFF - UNAGI AND FOIE GRAS WITH APPLE BALSAMIC

These two fuckers absolutely belong together. It may seem a bit like shooting fish in a barrel, two great, tasty ingredients together for a cheffy show-off extravaganza. And that would be fair enough, I suppose it is a bit like that, but to me this is an example of how the east and the west meld seamlessly. Foie gras has been used in Japan since they began importing it, circa mid-1960s, so although it's not something we view as typically Japanese, it's been kicking around for a while. I'm sure I'm not the only one who's served up this killer combo. It's probably been done to death somewhere in Japan but I haven't seen it so I feel like I can take some credit for this.

My thoughts on foie gras: it's had some really bad press and deservedly so. However, in the wild, geese and ducks instinctively smash a shit-ton of food ahead of their migrating journey south for the winter. They smash it so hard that their livers wind up the lovely fatty thing we call foie gras. I will never buy shitty foie gras that's been reared poorly or treated badly. Instead, I buy from ethical producers, such as the ones that I've visited in France that let their ducks and geese roam free for most of their lives.

Try to marinate your foie gras in den miso (see page 244) one day ahead of whatever dish you're making, as it adds a sweetness and umami kick that no proud Michelin starred fancy pants cook has ever served me. You'll need about 30ml for the amount of foie gras below.

SERVES 2 AS PART OF A MULTI-COURSE MENU

35–40g foie gras
30ml den miso (see page 244), optional (see introduction above)
150g unagi kabayaki (sweet grilled eel, available from Japanese shops), cut into 6 even pieces
30ml unagi sauce (see page 251)
grapeseed oil, for frying

For the apple balsamic

150ml balsamic vinegar (doesn't have to be top-grade balsamic)
200ml apple juice
1 Granny Smith apple, cut into 6 wedges

To serve

½ Granny Smith apple
puffed soba (see page 248)
pickled grapes

If you have time (and want to impress), marinate your foie gras in the den miso the day before you want to serve.

To make the apple balsamic, simmer all the ingredients in a pan for 20–25 minutes over a medium heat. Allow to cool, strain, then set aside.

Heat a salamander (top heat grill) or ordinary grill. Brush the unagi pieces with half the unagi sauce and cook under the salamander, until well caramelised. Brush with the other half of the sauce during grilling.

Next, heat a non-stick pan over a high heat and add a few drops of grapeseed oil.

Wipe the den miso (if used) from the foie gras, and add to the pan. Cook over a high heat and allow the foie gras to colour well, and then flip over. Brown well on the other side, too. Remove from the pan and set aside in a warm place (near a hot stove is perfect) to soften up.

Arrange the foie gras and unagi overlapping on a plate, lunch box or whatever you think is funky, and drizzle with the apple balsamic. Grate your Granny Smith apple, skin on, and make a mound of it on the side of the plate. Finally sprinkle with the puffed soba and drop some gari (pickled grapes), on the side as a refresher, once you're done.

Get down!

MOUNTAIN POTATO BUNS WITH MISO YAKI RABBIT

You don't often see rabbit feature in Japanese cuisine, hardly ever I'd say, if not never. When my mate Mike (Morton) Brown and I opened our pan-Asian joint in France, nearly a million years ago now, we featured a Thai green curry of rabbit. The Frenchies nearly shat themselves - Bah, no, you cannot! I fucking can, and you're gonna love it - and they did. Blinkers off, Frenchies! It takes a naive 25-year-old Aussie backpacker to rudely upset the comfortable and well-established Savoie region's restaurant scene. Anyway, after France it was London for me and I still had a hankering for the rabbit. Here is what I began to play around with...

SERVES 4

For the mountain potato bread

2 medium-sized potatoes (anything that's good for mashing), peeled and cut into 3–4cm chunks

150g yama imo root (sticky mountain potato), grated (this can be hard to find, but you can normally source it pre-grated and frozen from Japanese shops or online, and then it's called tororo)

1 teaspoon sea salt

20g salted butter, softened

100g plain flour, plus extra to dust

80g clarified butter

For the rabbit

300ml den miso (page 244)

2 green chillies, roughly chopped

1 whole rabbit, gutted and cute fluffy tail removed

2 litres dashi (see page 245)

5cm piece kombu

For the chilli-miso-truffle sauce

50ml den miso (see page 244)

2 handfuls of frozen spinach

1 medium chilli, roughly chopped

4 teaspoons Japanese rice vinegar

truffle oil, to taste

To prepare the rabbit, combined the miso and chillies, and spread all over the rabbit. Cover and leave to marinate in the fridge for 24 hours.

Fire up the barbie and barbecue the rabbit until well-coloured. (You do this to impart some barbecue-flavour into the rabbit not to cook it.)

Heat the oven to 190°C/170°C fan/Gas Mark 5. Put the whole rabbit in a deep ovenproof dish, pour over the dashi, adding the kombu too. Cover with foil and cook in the oven for 40 minutes.

Handpick the meat from the rabbit bones and get hipster with it (meaning, you're making pulled rabbit). Mix about 90ml of the liquid from the dish with the meat and chill, covered, until needed.

Meanwhile, make the chilli-miso-truffle sauce. Blend all the ingredients vigorously until fine, and then pass through a muslin-lined sieve and set aside until needed.

To make the bread, first cook the potatoes in a pan of boiling water for about 20 minutes, or until soft. Drain well and then mash. Stir in the grated yamo imo and mix well. Stir in the salt and butter, then finally fold in the flour until well incorporated.

Turn out onto a floured surface and knead for 5 minutes, until a tight, elastic dough forms. Wrap the dough in clingfilm and rest for a minimum of 1 hour.

When ready to use, roll the dough out into a log about 4–5cm in diameter. Cut off 35–40g chunks and roll out again to make 2cm-thick discs.

Heat the clarified butter in a non-stick frying pan and pan-fry the bread discs over a medium-low heat for 4 minutes on each side, until golden all over.

Now you're ready to build your rabbit sandwiches.

Place a 50–60g dollop of the chilled 'pulled' rabbit on one of the mountain potato breads, sandwich it with another bread and press down. Cut into quarters and serve one sandwich per person, drizzled with chilli-miso-truffle sauce.

BUTTER FRIED DOVER SOLE WITH SPICY SHISO PONZU

I can't avoid a well-cooked Dover sole. Sole meunière is one of my favourite dishes ever. It's unavoidable for me, that rich, nutty butter, the texture, the odd caper or two - it's last meal stuff. This dish came about when I was sweating it out on the line at Nobu in Park Lane. Drew Nierporent, legendary New York restaurateur and Nobu partner, had just landed in town and as usual came in to say hi. He asked me to take care of his menu but he wanted Dover sole. I thought, in the heat of it (we used to rock 400/500 covers for dinner back then) he must be feeling like sole meunière - fuck, I would be - and this is going to be my starting point. I jazzed it up with a salsa that I'd been tinkering with, something fresh, zesty with a hint of chilli and a double whack of shiso to steer it back towards something Japanese-y. It worked, it fucking worked! It was one of those moments when you know you've nailed it. It went onto be a special, then on to the menu, even Nobu-san had a crack at making it for one of his books.

The sauce also works with steamed green veg, with langoustines hot off the barbie, or as a dip for salmon sashimi or whatever else you have - it's the 'cheat' sauce.

SERVES 2 AS PART OF A MULTI-COURSE MENU (BUT I COULD EASILY EAT ONE OF THESE ON MY OWN)

1 skinless Dover sole, approx. 400g or so

1 litre rapeseed oil for deep-frying

1 tablespoon grapeseed oil,

20g plain flour

60g best-quality salted butter, diced into
  1cm × 1cm chunks

spicy shiso ponzu (see page 249)

sea salt and freshly ground black pepper

It's a total joy to fillet a Dover sole as it's a flat fish and has 4 fillets, 2 on the top and 2 on the underside. Once the skin is off you'll see the layout much more clearly. Run the knife down the centre and, pressing the knife against the bone, work the fillet away in smooth, longish swipes of the knife. (You can check out YouTube for videos on how to do this.) Do this for each fillet. Obviously, you could ask your fish bloke to do it for you too!

Keep the bone – it's tasty and crunchy. Cut away the head and whack the bone straight into the fryer and deep-fry it at 180°C/350°F until it's golden. Remove and drain on kitchen paper. Set aside.

When you're nearly ready to serve, heat a non-stick frying pan over a medium heat and add 1 tablespoon of grapeseed oil. Lightly season the sole fillets with salt and pepper on both sides. Now, run the fillets through the flour, coat well, then shake off any excess flour.

The fillets will appear to have a convex or outwardly curved side; place this into the pan, one piece at a time. Give the pan a gentle shake to ensure no sticking is going down. After about 1½ minutes, add the chunks of butter, spreading them evenly around the pan and giving the pan some more shaking action. Cook for 40–50 seconds. Your fish should start taking on a sexy golden colour; if it hasn't you could raise the heat a little or wait a bit longer.

So, once it's golden, turn off the heat, flip the fish over and give it a last little shake around. Allow the fillets to rest for 30 seconds and let the residual heat finish gently cooking the underside.

Plate 'em up and drizzle your sauce over. Make sure that you don't forget to include the crunchy bone – break it into pieces to make it easier to share. (Be careful though, a bone is still a bone and you'll need to watch out.)

LOBSTER AND CHIPS

Lobsters used to be posh. They can still be fairly expensive little buggers, but times have changed. Dressing up in your best gut-hugging suit coat, sitting nicely and eating it politely in front of monkey nailers isn't how you'll see lobsters being devoured these days. Lobsters have gone street, they show up in food trucks, pop-ups, and burger joints, and hipsters on bicycles serve them in vintage saxophones with wangberry chutney...

I fucking love chips too - who isn't partial to the lengthy array of chips, crisps, triple-cooked chips, skinny fries and all the rest? You could use whatever you like that's in season to make the chips - for example, Jerusalem artichoke, parsnip or sweet potato. I love beet chips - look out for the red, the golden and the candy cane.

It's a far cry from Japan but this yuzu egg sauce and my kombu-soy-butter cooking process inject the dish with a whole load of Japanese umami. Use whatever root veg you like to make your chips as well as some skinny potato fries. I cook the lobster sous vide style, you can get away with a pan, a low flame or hob and some babysitting.

SERVES 2

1 live lobster, approx. 450g

2 tablespoons light soy sauce

2cm piece kombu

20g good-quality salted butter

20ml sake

30g ginger, thinly sliced

2 spring onion lengths, mostly the
    white part

For the chips

½ root veg of choice (parsnip, beetroot,
    artichoke etc.)

1 litre rapeseed oil, for deep-frying

½ potato (ask your local grower for the
    best potatoes for chips, you'll need to
    change varieties throughout the year as
    they go in and out of season)

To serve

yuzu-truffle-egg sauce (see page 124),
    omit the truffle, or not

finely chopped chives

Knock the lobster out by freezing it for a couple of hours, and then blanch it in boiling water for 2 minutes, then chill in iced water for 2 minutes. Remove the shell and cut the meat into pieces that would be easily managed with chopsticks (bite-sized chunks). Combine the lobster meat with the remaining ingredients.

Heat your sous vide machine to 56°C/130°F, whack the lobster and stuff into a vacuum bag or 2 zip-lock plastic bags and seal. Submerge into the water for 12 minutes – weigh it down if it's a floater.

Peel and use a mandoline to thinly slice your veg of choice into rounds. Heat the oil in a fryer or large pan to 160°C/320°F, and fry until crunchy. They may not be 100 per cent crispy when you pull them out, but that's fine. Put them on a tray lined with kitchen paper and into an oven at its lowest setting. After 1 hour they will be just right but keep them in the oven until you need them.

To make the chips, cut the potatoes into longish pieces, approximately 5–6cm long and 2mm thick. Wash, drain well and dry.

Heat the oil to 140°C/275°F and cook for 2 minutes until the chips are soft and soggy. Remove and drain well. Increase the heat to 180°C/350°F and drop your soggy chips in and cook until golden and crisp.

Once the lobster is cooked, cut open the bag, drain the juices, ginger and kombu, and plate the lobster with the chips and yuzu egg sauce in a pot on the side.

You could go total street vendor on your guests and serve this up in greaseproof paper, or risk a dirty newspaper. Scatter your warm, buttery, umami-rich lobster around your street-cred paper, scatter your chips about, then drizzle with your sauce and maybe some chopped chives if using.

SMOKEY PORK GYOZA WITH SESAME DIP

Cured and tea-smoked pork neck is the killer filler for these little fuckers. Gyoza making is the one thing that used to get our chefs into fierce competition mode. The objective was to make as many tiny folds on the dumplings as neatly as possible. My whole thing was that the deep-frozen gyoza that you buy in the freezer section of Japanese grocers were imperfect, having only four or five folds. As skilful chefs we ought to be able to make it look much finer, so it was game on.

Plan ahead with this one. Your pork neck needs a solid 12 hours' curing time. And I personally think you need to give the smoked meat an overnight spell in the fridge to let the astringent, strong, overly smoky flavour settle.

SERVES 2 AS PART OF A MULTI-COURSE MENU

8 gyoza skins (they come frozen in large packs, defrost only what you need and they'll last for ages)
light olive oil, for frying
2 spring onions, chopped
½ red chilli, cut into chunks
2 splashes sesame oil

For the pork neck
200g pork neck
100g bacon cure (see page 111)
smoke mix (see page 104)

For the sesame dip
140g Japanese sesame paste (tahini is ok if you're stuck and don't mind it tasting like hippy ponzu sauce)
100ml ponzu sauce (see page 247)
35g caster sugar
2 splashes of roasted sesame oil

For the gyoza mix
2 lengths spring onions – green and white bits, chopped, washed and dried
1 teaspoon roasted sesame oil
1 teaspoon toasted white sesame seeds
1 teaspoon chilli-garlic paste
1½ teaspoons grated ginger
2½ teaspoons light soy sauce
1 egg
sea salt and freshly ground black pepper

Wash your pork, drain and dry it. Rub thoroughly with the bacon cure, and pack it on. Refrigerate for 12 hours. Wash off the cure and drain well.

When ready to smoke, heat a wok or large pan and follow the directions on page 104. Place the pork on a rack and place over the smoke, then cover well. Hot smoke for 4 minutes on each side.

Remove from the heat and set the pork aside to cool to room temperature. Place on a plate and cover with clingfilm, then refrigerate for a good 5 hours or more.

To make the dip simply blend the ingredients with 50ml of water until smooth and keep refrigerated until required.

When you're ready to make the gyoza, mince the pork neck in a mincer (or chop by hand for a coarser texture and one hell of an aching hand). Slip on some food-safe gloves and massage the smoked pork neck with the rest of the gyoza mix ingredients until it's all well combined. Take a small teaspoonful and pan-fry it to test the seasoning, Fry, eat, taste. Yum? No, adjust the seasoning as necessary. If it's ok let's carry on…

Make sure the pork mix is well chilled before and during the process, and when the gyoza skins are not required, keep them wrapped in a damp cloth or tea towel to stop them drying out.

Take a gyoza skin and place a good dollop (about 25g) of the chilled pork mix into the centre. Dip your finger into cold water and run it around the rim of the skin. Lift the gyoza in your left hand and, using your moist finger, spread the mixture evenly. Starting at the bottom left corner pinch the dough together, then continue to pull the dough closest to you over to the left, making small folds. Pinch each fold to seal it shut – 8–10 folds is cool. Be a maniac once you've nailed the technique and try to beat my 30-ish!

To cook the gyoza, heat a non-stick pan and lightly oil the base with light olive oil. Press the flat side of the gyoza into the hot pan and let it sizzle away over a medium-high heat for 2–3 minutes, until it becomes golden – lift at intervals to check.

At this stage, pour in enough water to come halfway up the gyoza (pan size and batch size will determine the exact quantity of water you need). Immediately cover with a lid and cook over a high heat, until the water evaporates. Remove the lid and allow the base to get crunchy again, another 30 seconds.

Toss in some chopped spring onions and chunks of red chilli along with a couple of splashes of sesame oil. Once the base has become crunchy again, quickly toss the gyozas, spring onion and chilli around the pan a couple of times then tip into your serving bowl. Serve 'em up with the sesame dip.

CURRIED CONGEE WITH LANGOUSTINES

This is soul-enriching stuff. It is for any time of the day but often breakfast. It has a thousand possible toppings or seasonings and it's a big gluggy bowl of extremely over-cooked rice!

I first encountered congee when I was 19. I was working in a hotel kitchen which would have inspired the producers of *Ramsay's Kitchen*

Nightmares to pack it in. Anyway, I bravely ate a big bowl of congee each day and not only survived to tell the tale, but also changed my breakfast routine forever.

This is less of a breakfast version, but you'd probably want to eat this as a light supper, or, if you're like me, any time is congee time!

SERVES 2 AS PART OF A MULTI-COURSE MENU

4 langoustines, shelled and deveined
a splash of dark soy sauce
a dash of sake
a dash of mirin
small knob of salted butter

For the red hot umami oil

80g dried red chilli flakes
2 garlic cloves
10g dried shrimp
5cm piece kombu
5cm length Parmesan rind
a small handful of katsuobushi (bonito
   flakes)
1 small red pepper, deseeded and cut
   into small dice approx. 2mm × 2mm
6 small red bird's eye chillies
300ml light olive oil
60ml toasted sesame oil

For the curried congee

160g sushi rice
120g cauliflower, cut into small florettes
1½ tablespoons curry powder
6cm piece kombu
2–3cm piece ginger, halved
2 litres chicken stock
light soy sauce, to taste
roasted sesame oil, to taste
sea salt and freshly ground black pepper,
   to taste

To serve

pork scratchings, chopped (see page 27)
2 spring onions, chopped
2cm piece ginger, finely grated

First make the umami oil. Combine all the ingredients in a pan and cook over a low heat for 45 minutes. The oil should be at about 65°C/150°F. Allow to cool, and then refrigerate for a good 6 hours minimum. The next day, reheat the oil to approximately 40°C/100°F, then strain well. Decant into an airtight glass jar and refrigerate (it will last a good while!).

It's pretty simple to make the curried congee; you want to overcook the rice until it becomes kind of like a stodgy porridge. To do this, whack the rice, cauliflower, curry powder, kombu, ginger and stock into a pot – bigger than you think you need. Get it over a high heat and bring to the boil. Reduce the heat to medium and cook for 30–40 minutes, stirring often as it burns easily. It will become really thick and there shouldn't be any rice granules. You may need to add more stock or even water and continue to cook, covered, until the rice is totally broken down. Season with a dash of light soy sauce, roasted sesame oil and a bit of salt and pepper. It doesn't need to be mega-seasoned now as you will be adding other elements to it, which will balance the flavour out.

For the langoustines, try to find whole, live ones. Google it – there will be some nut out there willing to ice them up and send them via FedEx. If not, scour the world for the best-quality langoustine meat. Again, fresh is best, frozen is death. This recipe is intended for use with vac bags, a vac pack machine and a water circulator – posh bugger, I hear you mutter, well that's where you're wrong. Here's household botch job lesson number one. Those of you with all the fancy kit will know how to adapt this back to big-tall-hat-chef level; or will you?

First, fill a deep saucepan with water and heat to around 55°C/130°F. Next, get some zip-lock plastic bags and put one inside the other. Put your shelled and deveined langoustine tails into the inner bag; lay them flat, side by side, making sure they don't overlap. Add the dark soy sauce, sake, mirin and the butter. Push as much air out of the bags as possible, then zip them up. Slide the bag into the warm water; you'll need to weigh it down with a small brick or something else that's far more suitable, like a plate. Leave the langoustines in the water for about 12 minutes if they are big plump ones. If they are scrawny little buggers, cook them for about 4 minutes.

Now you're ready to roll. Give your congee one last taste to check that it is lightly seasoned. Pour the congee into a deep bowl. Top with the langoustines; keep the juices in the bag for later. Scatter the pork scratchings all around, along with the chopped spring onions and finely grated ginger. You may even want to add a drizzle of the langoustine cooking juices. Serve with a little red hot umami oil on the side, unless you're a total nut and in that case whack it on and let the chilli madness take over your brain.

DELUXE CHICKEN KATSU WITH CAFÉ DE PARIS BUTTER

Katsu cooking - you know it right? Panko crumbed and golden fried. Pork and chicken are the common ones, served with a plate of shredded cabbage, mustard, lemon steamed rice and tonkatsu sauce = brilliant! Another classic is katsu chopped up and served with a Japanese curry - dirty, but good dirty!

A pork katsu sando (sandwich) is probably my favourite though. I once ate this at a run of the mill, non-descript shopping arcade in Tokyo, it was blindingly good. It's mad how something that is seemingly so simple can get you buzzing. So after that, my shopping mall-mecca-moment, I started to think about how I would like to serve 'my' katsu. Weirdness flowed, as it does, but the one thing that seemed plausible was Café de Paris butter. On a steak with fries it can put me into a trance. Death row shit - you bet.

So, here it is, chicken breast fried and served with butter. You thought Japanese food was all about purity? You thought wrong, guilty pleasures are universal!

SERVES 2 DIRTY BUGGERS

1 plump corn-fed, free-range, best-reared, loved chicken breast
1 litre rapeseed oil, for deep-frying
20g plain flour
1 egg, beaten
130g Japanese panko breadcrumbs sea salt and freshly ground black pepper

For the Café de Paris butter

90g unsalted butter
1 teaspoon ketchup
½ teaspoon Dijon mustard
5g capers
1 tablespoon shallots, sliced
½ teaspoon parsley, roughly chopped
½ teaspoon chives, roughly chopped
a small pinch of majoram, roughly chopped
a small pinch of dill, roughly chopped
a small pinch of thyme, roughly chopped
¼ teaspoon tarragon, roughly chopped
½ **small** garlic clove, sliced
a small pinch of rosemary, chopped
1 anchovy
a dash of Worcestershire sauce
a small pinch of cayenne pepper
a large pinch of curry powder
¼ teaspoon paprika
2 black peppercorns
¼ teaspoon sea salt
1 teaspoon each orange zest and juice
1 teaspoon each lemon zest and juice
½ teaspoon brandy
½ teaspoon Madeira wine

To serve

½ lemon, cut into wedges
shredded cabbage

To make the butter, combine all the ingredients except the orange and lemon juices, brandy and Madeira. Let this sit for 24 hours at room temperature and then blitz in a food processor along with the citrus zest and juices and the alcohol. Tip the mixture onto a sheet of clingfilm and roll into a 4cm log, wrap and store in the refrigerator or freeze until firm. Cut off slices as needed – the butter will keep for months in the freezer and up to a week or so in the fridge.

For the katsu, make a cut in the thickest part of the breast, so that you even the overall thickness out. Fold out the part you've just cut – you now have a flatter, wider breast.

Heat the oil in a fryer or large pan to 180°C/350°F.

Season the chicken breast well with salt and pepper and then toss it in the flour. Run the breast through the egg to coat it well and then press it into the breadcrumbs. With good coarse crumbs you need only do this once, but if the crumbs are too fine you'll need to repeat the process and double crumb.

Deep-fry the chicken for about 2½ minutes, then remove with a perforated scoop and drain well on kitchen paper. Slice into 1cm strips, and serve alongside the lemon, cabbage and 2 or 3 dollops of gently melted Café de Paris butter.

INTO THE STEAM

ONSEN EGGS WITH TRUFFLE SALT

Also known as onsen tamago (hot spring egg), I thought this was a killer idea. Grab a basket of eggs and go sit in a hot spring for half an hour, get out and your breakfast is right there. Multi-tasking with ease! Don't even think about taking a box of eggs in your household bath – you'll be there a long time before getting out with uncooked eggs (I think, I'm not admitting to trying it out!). Check the recipe for Buta no Kakuni (see page 165) where I serve it with slow-cooked pork belly. Truffles don't go badly with this either.

egg/s

mix made of 4 parts dashi (see page 245), 1 part dark soy sauce and 1 part mirin (it's typical to get given recipes in parts by Japanese chefs – I think it's really useful as you can scale the quantities you need)

To serve, optional

potato crisps (thinly slice ½ potato, wash and dry well, then fry at 140°C/275°F until golden)

sautéed spinach

truffle salt

Traditionally, the eggs would be cooked in a spring that's around 70°C/160°F, a temperature that would also cook humans. Onsens can range from as manageable, and possibly a little cool, 20°C/70°F to around 100°C/210°F. I'd suggest one for the eggs and one for the humans.

Or, for a far less hassle-filled version, set your water bath to 63°C/145°F and drop your egg/s in for 1 hour. (To maintain this heat you can add a little cold water as you go.) With one gentle tap the shell will crack open and you can easily pull the two parts of the shell away to expose your plump, just-set 'onsen egg'. Serve in dashi-soy with a garnish of potato crisps, truffle salt or sautéed spinach.

HOT SAUNA POUSSIN

Wouldn't it be romantic if the recipe originated out of a steamy sauna nestled high up on a Japanese mountain? Outside, the snow has been gently falling and is now three feet deep. The poussin is marinated and ready to hit the oven in time for dinner when suddenly the oven goes out and there is no way to get these lovely soy-marinated dinner birds cooked. But wait, we left the sauna on, and it's red-lining at a deadly 200°C/400°F. The birds are rushed out to the cedar hotbox and the rest is history...

Wake up, snap out of it, this nonsensical daydream didn't happen (at least I don't think it did). No smoky sauna hotbox is required. It's as simple as barbecuing your poussin wrapped in sugita, which is a thinly planed cedarwood used to impart that sauna-like cedar scent to foods. (You can also grill whatever you want on top of it for 'sugita-yaki'; prawns, scallops, veg are placed atop water-soaked sugita, then dropped on a rack over hot coals.) The scent it gives off is fucking outstanding. If you can manage to get your sugita going at the table on a mini-barbecue, then you'll blow your guests' minds, even possibly smoke them to death if you screw it up by allowing it to catch fire. I'm taking no responsibility on this one! You'll need a large dollop of common sense if you're thinking of trying this at home.

SERVES 2, AS PART OF A MULTI-COURSE MENU

1 poussin, thigh bone removed

4 tablespoons dark soy sauce

4 tablespoons mirin

4 tablespoons sake

8cm piece ginger, sliced in half

8cm length spring onion, including green and white part, sliced in half

chilli-miso-truffle sauce (see page 173), to serve, optional

Equipment

1 sheet sugita (cedarwood) (this can be hard to source, but specialist Japanese suppliers should stock it. Alternatively, ask someone at your local hardware store to thinly plane some cedarwood for you instead.)

First, rub the poussin with the dark soy sauce, mirin and sake. Leave for 2 hours to marinate, and then drain away the marinade.

Soak the sheet of sugita in water for 20 minutes.

Place the ginger and spring onion slices on the inner sides of the poussin, Drain the sugita and use it to wrap the poussin tightly. Secure well with the string.

Fire up the barbecue. Cook the wrapped poussin over a gentle flame for 20 minutes or so, until the sugita is well charred.

Carefully unwrap the poussin (the steam will be hot), squirt with the chilli-miso-truffle sauce (or serve it on the side), if using, and enjoy.

JAPANESE MUSHROOMS GRILLED IN HOBA LEAF AND SERVED WITH CREAMY SEA URCHIN SAUCE

Hoba leaves are the leaves from the magnolia plant. In Japan, you'll see both dried and wet versions of them available. Personally, I'm a fan of the dried ones; they give off a brilliant scent when heat is applied, which then scents the food being cooked on them. Before using these, you'll need to soak them in water so that they don't burn, or if you're wrapping them all the way around something for steaming, likewise, and they'll become malleable. Other ingredients that go brilliantly cooked atop hoba are duck breast with some orange and miso, scallops, tofu and sesame; and, this recipe, which is one of my favourites, is mixing mushrooms and rice and serving atop the leaf.

If you can, grill this in front of your guests. We have small charcoal barbecues at the restaurant which we send out to the table. Aside from the odd smoke detector incident it's a killer way to let the guests experience what hoba grilling is about.

SERVES 2

a splash of light olive oil

150g mixed Japanese mushrooms (or even your local variety), thinly sliced if medium, but if small just cut in half

10g salted butter

1 garlic clove, thinly sliced

2 hoba leaves, soaked for about 20 minutes in cold water

For the sea urchin sauce

¼ onion

1 garlic clove, peeled and chopped

10g salted butter

80ml sake

100g best-quality sea urchin, removed from the shell

80ml dashi (see page 245)

20ml light soy sauce

2 teaspoons mirin

squeeze of lemon juice, approx. ¼ lemon

sea salt and freshly ground black pepper

First make the sauce. Sauté the onion and garlic in the butter, until they become translucent. Add the sake and boil for about 2 minutes to reduce the sauce by half.

Blend the onion and sake mixture with the sea urchin, dashi, soy sauce and mirin, and add a squeeze of lemon juice. Test the seasoning and perhaps add a pinch of salt or an extra drop of light soy if you fancy a little more saltiness. Leave to one side until ready to serve. It's best enjoyed at room temperature.

Heat a pan with a little splash of light olive oil and sauté the mushrooms with the butter and garlic until cooked through and lightly coloured.

Spread the mushrooms on top of the hoba leaves, then cook in any of the following ways:

1. Place them over medium hot coals.
2. Heat your oven to the max and heat them this way for about 1½ minutes.
3. Put then under a hot salamander.

All these methods work fine, but my favourite is the barbecue. Simply pour over the sauce and serve.

Note: If you want a version without the sea urchin, then use a little miso sauce, gorgonzola piccante, pine nuts and a squeeze of lemon in place of the sea urchin, dashi, soy sauce and mirin.

JAPANESE CURRY-STYLE SHORT RIBS

Japanese curry has become a comfort food for me. It was always being cooked up for the staff meal by the sushi chefs and every time I'd go and take some without them knowing. (They were very protective at times.) When you were totally knackered from split shift after split shift after hangover, turning to a bowl of curry and rice was like a warm soft blanket from childhood.

Guess I'm not the only one who takes both sustenance and reassurance from this type of Anglo-Indian curry: the Japanese Navy are also curry lovers. (It was actually introduced to Japan by the Brits. We should be thankful the Brits didn't introduce the Japanese to cricket, too. You know they would be perfect at it and kick our asses.)

Japanese curry can be found in three main forms: curry pan, a kind of curry-stuffed bread; topped with crumbled pork or chicken; or simply with root vegetables on rice, like this version.

SERVES 2

rapeseed oil, for frying
1 large white onion
5 garlic cloves, peeled and thinly sliced
2 bone-in rack of short rib
1 litre chicken stock
1 red apple, peeled, cored and
 diced small
3cm piece kombu
300g Japanese curry sauce mix (such as
 S&B Golden Curry Medium/Hot)
1 medium carrot, sliced into 2cm rounds
 or thin batons
2 chunks daikon radish, peeled and diced

To serve
baby onions
clarified butter
a splash of mirin
a splash of sake
steamed short-grain rice

Heat the oil in a large pan and sauté the onion and garlic for about 5 minutes, until they are soft but not coloured.

Heat a separate pan and heavily season the ribs with salt and pepper before adding them to the hot pan to brown. (We have our robata cranked up all the time so we brown the meat on it – it's a fantastic smoky option.) Once the meat is browned, add it to the pan with the onion and garlic, and then add the chicken stock, apple and kombu.

Break up the Japanese curry sauce mix by hand, whisk it up with 1 litre of water then pour this into the pan.

Cover the pan, heat the curry to 83°C/180°F and cook for around 3 hours, until the meat is falling off the bone. Add the carrot and daikon at the halfway point. Check from time to time, stirring, to make sure the curry hasn't dried out or burnt. If the liquid is reducing at an alarming rate top it up with water.

When the meat falls away easily from the bone and breaks up if you squash a teaspoon into it, it's done.

Now, you could get stuck into it immediately, or what's best is to let it cool and let the flavours develop. Stews and braises always taste better if left for an hour or more after cooking.

I finish my version with baby onions, simply sautéed in clarified butter and finished with a light splash of both mirin and sake.

Serve it up on hot, steamy rice. Never look back…

TEAPOT SOUP WITH PRAWNS, MUSHROOMS AND YUZU SKIN

This is a bit of a classic. It's called 'dobin mushi' and it is such a brilliant idea. You fill your teapot with a classic Japanese clear soup (a bit like a consommé in Western cuisine and a bit not as well), then load in some garnishes that will not only be nice to eat later but can also add to the flavour whilst the soup is heating up. Prawns, mushrooms and yuzu zest are classics for obvious reasons, so I am sticking to them. Want to make it a little more fancy? Use cep mushrooms, or Japanese maitake mushrooms. Of course, the addition of shaved truffle is killer.

MAKES ENOUGH FOR 1

180ml dashi (see page 245)

40ml sake

2 pinches of sea salt

30ml light soy sauce (never use dark for this as it makes it a shitty colour)

1–2 prawns (depending on how many will fit comfortably in your teapot), shells removed and deveined

15g mushrooms of your choice, or a mixture

2 long strands of yuzu skin

green veg of choice, for garnishing (shelled broad beans if in season are good)

Into the teapot it all goes…

Crank your steamer up and place the teapot, with its lid secured, inside the steamer. Pop the lid on your steamer and allow it to heat through for about 10 minutes. (If your steamer is set over a really fierce heat, then 8 minutes should do it.) Take the teapot out and test that it is piping hot and the prawns and mushrooms are cooked through.

Serve with a bowl on the side, a spoon and some chopsticks to retrieve the garnishes. Easy peasy, etc.

CLASSIC CHAWAN MUSHI TOPPED WITH SEA URCHIN AND SPICY `SILVER SAUCE`

This is basically a very lightly steamed savoury custard. The base is dashi and eggs seasoned with light soy. Toppings can vary but by far this is my favourite. I've even played about with the base mix, trying to infuse flavours, carefully adding purées, and although some have worked, some have been total fucking disasters. Verdict: keep the base simple, and vary your toppings.

This is mostly served as a hot dish. In fact, the finest versions of this are so soft they are almost runny like a soup. I prefer chawan mushi to be a little more firm than this, it's still quite soft and in no way rubbery, like some other egg-set creations. If you nail it, chawan mushi is soft and silky. Light as air to eat, yet packed with umami. It's odd, ethereal and captivating and then all of a sudden it's gone, like it was never there. Here's how you do it...

Note: it's really common to have measurements given in the form of parts as opposed to grams/litres etc. for something like this. For a very safe version of this recipe, make 2 parts dashi to 1 part whole egg rather than the 2.5 parts dashi that I use below.

MAKES 2

1 part egg
1 tablespoon light soy sauce
a pinch of sea salt
2.5 parts dashi (see page 245) (for 1 egg, this should be about 125ml)

For the silver sauce

80ml dashi (see page 245)
5g kudzu powder (Japanese arrowroot)
2 teaspoons light soy sauce
a splash of sake
a pinch of flaked sea salt

For the topping

2 plump sushi-grade pieces sea urchin
2 tiny dots of chilli-garlic paste from a jar, or other spicy condiment of your choice
1 teaspoon finely sliced spring onion, washed and dried
½ teaspoon finely grated ginger

First, beat the egg, soy sauce and salt with the dashi – do not use a whisk as this will aerate the mixture and we want to keep it dense. Instead, gently break up the egg with a pair of household chopsticks – it takes longer but c'est la vie.

Strain the mixture through a medium-coarse sieve into a bowl. You will cause a few bubbles to appear while doing this, so slam the bowl down on the work surface a few times until the bubbles surface and pop. Set aside until required.

Next, make the silver sauce – so called because it kinda looks silver ... if you squint and look from a certain angle, in a certain light. (Apologies Nick Cave.) Heat the dashi in a saucepan to 80°C/175°F. Mix the kudzu in water to form a firm paste, whisk into the dashi and cook for 1 minute over a high heat – it needs to be just below boiling. Remove from the heat and season with light soy sauce, sake and salt. Keep hot while you prepare the remaining elements, and whisk just before use.

OK, so when it's required pour the dashi-egg mix into small bowls, cups or other funky pottery – roughly about 80–90ml per bowl/cup and if possible each with a lid. Loosely cover with the lid (or foil if necessary) and steam for about 12 minutes. Test to see if it's fully set, and, if not, continue to steam for a further minute at a time until it's set. It will be very wobbly and almost as if it's not set, but have a second glance – it may well be. It's going to be a brand new texture to some, so please double check before committing it to overcooking.

Once cooked, top each one with a piece of sea urchin, then pour over a couple of tablespoons worth of warm silver sauce. Finally give it a dot of chilli-garlic sauce, some spring onion and grated ginger. Truffle is a most welcome addition too, ohhh yeah!

SWEET

BANANA CREAM PIE WITH SAKE KASU ICE CREAM

Sometimes also known as banoffee pie, my banana cream pie is based on my first ever encounter with such a dessert when I was working in a small but very busy restaurant in Toronto, Canada. If I'm honest, and you know that means I'm going to be brutally honest, I thought this was a total fucking joke. An Americanised, home cook's creation, which is worthy of a truck-stop diner at best. And what pissed me off even more was that these chefs were so damn proud of it and the customers spoke about it as if this was a revelation. Jeeze, I was thinking that the truck drivers could come up with better, more innovative desserts than this. So there I was, each day as the kitchen wound down from the hustle and bustle, the heated arguments and the tense air of it all, finishing up with the constructing and plating of pie after pie. I'd do my best to refine it and make it a little more perfect than the head chef could (which wasn't hard - he had fingers like tree stumps and was pickled in whisky). But one day it happened - this is a much improved version.

The ice cream makes more than is needed here, but it can be eaten another time.

MAKES 6 PIES

3 bananas, roughly chopped, plus extra
    slices to decorate
caster sugar, to dust
puffed soba (see page 248)

For the sake kasu ice cream
180g sake kasu, broken into pieces
60ml sake
1 litre full-cream milk
40g trimoline
60g liquid glucose
300g double cream
200g caster sugar
70g milk powder

For the filo shell
120ml clarified butter, melted
180g caster sugar
200g filo pastry, cut into 15cm x
    15cm squares

For the tonka caramel
180g caster sugar
50g salted butter
300ml double cream
100g liquid glucose
5 tonka beans, finely grated
60g milk chocolate, chopped into
    small pieces

First make the ice cream. Soak the sake kasu in a bowl with the sake for 1 hour at room temperature and then blend until smooth.

In a pan, combine the milk, trimoline, glucose and cream. Bring to the boil.

In a separate bowl, combine the sugar, milk powder and the sake kasu mix, and mix together well. Pour into the milk mixture, whisk well, then strain. Leave to cool down and then churn until firm, which should take about 25 minutes in a decent ice cream machine. Freeze until required.

I use square metal moulds to make the pie shells, roughly about 8cm x 8cm, but if you have circles, triangles or even a muffin tin you'll be fine. First, brush your moulds with the clarified butter. Evenly coat the inside of the moulds with sugar and shake until well coated – remove any excess sugar and then set the moulds to one side.

Keep your filo covered with a lightly damp cloth so that it doesn't dry out – if it does you're screwed and you'll need new pastry. Lay down the first of your pastry squares, brush well with butter and lightly scatter sugar over the top (evenly), then place a second square on top and press them together so that they stick. Repeat this so you have 5 squares combined. Now pick up your buttery sheets and carefully line 1 of the moulds, gently pressing the pastry into the base and every corner if you're using a square mould. Repeat the process until all your moulds are lined and then refrigerate for 1 hour.

Preheat the oven to 180°C/160°C fan/Gas Mark 4 and bake the pastry moulds from cold for 15 minutes, until the pastry turns a dark golden colour.

Remove from the oven and run a paring knife between the pastry and the mould to prevent the pastry sticking to the mould once it cools. Allow them to cool in the moulds for 6–7 minutes (it should still be fairly warm) and then tip the moulds over and lift them away from the pastry cases. Store them on a wire rack in a cold dry place until required.

ingredients continued on page 210

recipe continued on page 210

In a pan, combine the milk, trimoline, glucose and cream, and bring to the boil.

In a separate bowl, combine the sugar and milk powder, and mix together well. Whisk this with the milk mixture and then strain. Leave to cool down. This is your base.

Work with 500ml of the ice cream base at a time, and pour it into your mixer with the whisk attachment fixed on. Whisk on speed 6 or 7 until it's foaming slightly.

Now it's dry ice time – you'll need about 100g per 500ml ice cream.

Smash up the dry ice in a tea towel – use a cricket bat or other solid wooden weapon – until you have small, fine pieces. Bit by bit, tip this into the whisking ice cream base mixture and after about 1½ minutes you will see it looking very foamy. Continue to add all the dry ice until it's incorporated – after 2 minutes you should have a firm, creamy soft serve.

Working quickly, scoop the ice cream into a piping bag with your favourite nozzle attachment (or just a star). Pipe the soft serve into the cones in a circular motion. They melt fairly fast so eat 'em up!

ICED RASPBERRY PARFAIT WITH BLACK SUGAR SYRUP

The inspiration for this comes from two separate parts of the planet. The syrup is a classic Japanese one named kuro mitsu and in summer it wouldn't be uncommon to see it generously poured over vanilla ice cream - such a brilliant, simple treat to sooth the hot and humid days during Japan's summers. The other part - the parfait - is from my mate Dave (Mungbean) Allen, back in western Australia. When we were apprentice chefs (he was my senior) he came up with a honey-nougat parfait with grapefruit - it was excellent and I always refer to it.

SERVES 10

1 gelatine leaf
75g caster sugar
225g honey
50g corn syrup
4 egg whites
250g raspberries, 150g roughly chopped
   and 100g halved
620g double cream, whipped to
   soft peaks
finely grated zest of 1 orange

For the kuro mitsu
100g muscovado sugar

To serve
a handful of raspberries
roasted walnuts, chopped

First, line a semi-deep tray or brownie tin (about 30cm × 20cm) with clingfilm.

Soak the gelatine leaf in a small bowl of cold water to soften for 5 minutes.

Cook the sugar, honey and corn syrup together in a pan until it reaches about 120°C/250°F.

Next, drain the gelatine and squeeze out any excess water. In the bowl of a standmixer, whisk the egg whites and soaked gelatine leaf until the egg whites are starting to foam. With the mixer on, slowly drizzle in the syrup, in a constant stream, until the syrup is all incorporated and the mixture stiff and shiny.

Remove the bowl from the mixer, add the raspberries, whipped cream and orange zest, and fold until evenly combined. Pour the mixture into the prepared tray and cover with clingfilm. Freeze for at least 3 hours, or until solid, before cutting.

To make the kuro mitsu, heat the sugar in a pan and cook gently, without stirring, until you have a dark sugar syrup – this should take about 5 minutes. Cool to room temperature before use.

Serve up 3 or 4 small blocks of the parfait per person and top with some more chopped or broken up raspberries and chopped roasted walnuts. Drizzle with plenty of kuro mitsu or serve it on the side.

ICED PASSION FRUIT AND SAKE PARFAIT

When I was a kid, we had passion fruit growing on the wire fence of the 'chook yard' (the place where we kept our chickens). I suppose I took it for granted that we had such amazing, ripe, organic (chook poo is a great fertiliser) and fairly sweet passion fruit on our doorstep. I don't think I'd ever eaten a store-bought number until I became an apprentice chef, when I first tasted mass-produced, sometimes-dry and not-very-sweet passion fruit. I mean, they should be slightly tangy but these things were more like a big spoonful of citric acid than a good passion fruit. What to do...?

I guess the moral of the story is to make an effort to source the best, sweetest and most well-grown passion fruit (the same goes for all sourcing really - this ought to be obvious, but I don't reckon it always happens).

I serve these as a kind of pre-dessert. Serve at least two per person as you can't stop at one.

MAKES AROUND 12 CUPS

1 gelatine leaf
150g caster sugar
400g honey
110g corn syrup
5 egg whites
60g sake kasu purée
500g cream, whipped
pulp from 8 passion fruits, keep 12 of the halves – wash and dry and set aside
ice cubes, to serve, optional

For the passion fruit kimi-yaki topping
5 egg whites
8 tablespoons caster sugar
80ml passoa (passion fruit liqueur)
1 teaspoon yuzu juice
1 tablespoon sake (unpasteurised if possible)

Equipment
blowtorch

Soak the gelatine leaf in a small bowl of cold water for 5 minutes.

Meanwhile, boil the sugar, honey and corn syrup in a pan until it reaches 120°C/250°F. Start to whip the egg whites in a large bowl when the sugar reaches about 85°C/185°F, and as soon as the sugar syrup reaches the magic 120°C/250°F, pour it over the whipping egg whites in a steady stream until well incorporated and you are left with a thickened, shiny meringue.

Remove the gelatine from the water and squeeze out the excess water; mix with the sake kasu purée, until completely dispersed. Fold this into the egg white mixture until combined and then fold in the whipped cream and passion fruit pulp.

Scoop the mixture into the cleaned passion fruit halves and pile it high. Freeze for at least 1½ hours.

For the passion fruit kimi-yaki topping, pick a pan that a stainless-steel bowl sits on top of neatly. Half-fill the pan with water and bring to the boil.

In the stainless-steel bowl, vigorously whisk all the ingredients until you achieve a pale, thick mixture. Set the bowl over the boiling water and continue to whisk until it has quadrupled in size. Remove from the heat and leave to cool.

To serve, remove the passion fruit cups from the freezer and allow to sit at room temperature for 2 minutes. Scoop a generous teaspoon of the passion fruit kimi-yaki topping over each cup and then gently blowtorch the topping. Serve up on a bed of ice to really impress.

SOBA ICE CREAM WITH CARAMELISED APRICOTS

Soba grain (aka buckwheat) makes killer ice cream – simply overcook it, blend it up and you're well on your way to a brilliant new ice cream flavour. I'm going to presume that not many people have made this before – if you have, get over it!

It goes without saying that using properly ripe apricots is best. If you can't source them, tinned apricots will do a reasonable job – in fact I'd rather tinned over unripe, tasteless apricots.

SERVES 4

For the soba ice cream
500ml gen mai cha ice cream base (see page 211)
300g soba grains (or use buckwheat grains if you can't source soba)

For the umeshu jelly
3 gelatine leaves
200ml umeshu (Japanese plum liqueur)

For the caramelised apricots
120ml unsalted butter
4–6 apricots, cut in half, stone removed
100g soft light brown sugar
60ml sake
40ml mirin
60ml umeshu

To serve
zest of 1 lime
toasted coconut flakes, optional

To make the ice cream, put the milk ice cream base and 200ml of water in a pan with the soba grains. Bring to the boil and cook for about 15 minutes, until very soft. (Japanese grains tend to cook really quickly.)

Pour through a fine sieve into a bowl, and then blend until smooth, adding a little of the cooking milk (just enough to get the blades of the blender cutting the grains and blending nicely).

Churn as per your ice cream maker's instructions. If you don't have an ice cream maker, see method on pages 211–213.

Next, make the umeshu jelly. Soak the gelatine leaves in a small bowl of water for 3–5 minutes, then drain and squeeze out any excess moisture. Line a 2mm-thick tray with clingfilm and then warm the umeshu to 65°C/150°F. Add the soaked gelatine and stir to dissolve. Pour the mix into the lined tray and chill for a minimum of 1 hour.

While this is chilling, prepare the apricots. In a non-stick pan, heat the butter until gently foaming. Arrange the apricots in the pan, flat side down, and allow them to colour a little, shaking your pan the whole time or they will stick like shit to a blanket.

Once the apricots are starting to colour, add the brown sugar, sake, mirin and umeshu and simmer over a medium-high heat until the apricots start to soften. Flip the apricots over and finish cooking through. Turn the heat up and allow the juices to thicken slightly. Remove from the heat and allow to cool for 5 minutes before serving.

To serve, divide the slightly warmed apricots so you have 2–3 halves per person, and add a large scoop of soba ice cream to the dish. Add some juices from the apricots and grate over some fresh lime zest, to decorate. Toasted coconut is a good addition, too.

WARM DONUTS WITH YUZU CURD

Fresh, hot donuts - what a great thing. A wonderful childhood memory, or so I thought. I can't for the life of me work out where the hell I would have had freshly made donuts as a kid in the part of the world where I come from. Maybe these were the ones I was yearning for when I ate the stale jam-filled whopper donuts from our local bakery. You'll notice two coatings here, matcha and sugar, and soba and sugar. Both are filled with yuzu curd, right before serving up. Do it too early and you'll see it all drip away. Fuck, even do it in front of the guests, why the hell not?!

MAKES ABOUT 40-50 DONUTS

1 litre rapeseed oil, for deep-frying

For the first mix
15g live yeast, dissolved in warm water
250g plain flour

For the second mix
15g live fresh yeast
200g full-cream milk, warmed to
    40°C/105°F
500g plain flour
25g caster sugar
80g butter, melted
120g egg yolks (approx. 8 eggs)
1 teaspoon sea salt

For the yuzu curd
½ gelatine leaf
180g unsalted butter, melted and cooled
    a little so it's slightly warm
150g sugar
100g yuzu juice
2 eggs

For the soba sugar
250g sugar
80g puffed soba (page 248)

For the matcha sugar
250g sugar
2 teaspoons matcha powder

To make the first mix, use a standmixer fitted with the dough hook attachment, and mix the yeast and flour together with 125ml of water, until well incorporated. Remove the dough from the mixer, cover in clingfilm and let it prove at room temperature for 2 hours until it's doubled in size.

For the second mix, dissolve the yeast in the warm milk and then set aside to cool. Mix the flour and sugar in a standmixer (again, using the dough hook attachment). Pour in the milk and yeast mixture, and combine well on speed 6 or 7.

Add the melted butter, egg yolks and salt, and mix well. Finally, add in the first mixture to this second mix and combine. Leave the combined dough in the fridge overnight or for a good 4–5 hours, minimum.

In the meantime, prepare the curd. Put the gelatine leaf in ice-cold water and set aside. Mix the rest of the ingredients in a heatproof bowl. Set the bowl over a pan of simmering water (make sure the bottom of the bowl doesn't touch the water) and cook quickly for 8–10 minutes, until the mixture thickens, then take off the heat and stir in the gelatine. Pour the mixture into a blender and blitz until the mixture turns a pale yellow colour. Pour into a bowl and chill in the fridge to set.

You can also use this time to prepare the sugar coatings. Blend together the sugar and puffed soba until fine, and then set aside. In a separate bowl, mix the sugar and matcha, and set this aside, too.

Once the dough has proved, divide the mix into 10g balls.

Heat your spanking clean oil in a fryer or large pan to 180°C/350°F, and fry the donuts in batches until golden, roughly about 3½–4 minutes, turning once. When you have fried the required amount of donuts, remove with a perforated scoop and allow them to briefly cool on kitchen paper for a max of 1 minute.

Poke a hole in the balls with the fat end of a chopstick. Pipe in as much yuzu curd as you can – make it overflow.

Roll half the balls in the soba sugar and the other half in the matcha sugar, coating them well. Plate up and sprinkle over more sugar on top and on the plate.

Eat fast, make more!

FRIED RASPBERRY ICE CREAM 'HARUMAKI' WITH BOOZY SHOCHU CHERRIES

This is a bit of a 'user-upper' kind of dish. I totally cheat and cut up little rectangles of the iced raspberry parfait on page 214, wrap it up in a sheet of feuilles de brick, refreeze for an hour or so, flash fry and voila! Also, I totally loved fried desserts as a kid - fried pineapple, fried banana and of course fried ice cream - all of which came from the local Chinese restaurant and probably the same deep-fat fryer where the majority of the main menu originated.

So, here we are - ice cream-based spring rolls ('harumaki' is the Japanese word for spring roll). This probably wouldn't work with your run of the mill, shop-bought ice cream - they have been developed to be perfectly scoopable and yet stable in less than ideal freezing conditions, but subject them to a deep-fryer and I reckon you'll have some seriously dangerous explosions going on. Stick to this recipe for the safest results.

SERVES 2

2 sheets feuilles de brick pastry

20g tempura flour

4 x 6cm x 2.5cm logs of iced raspberry parfait (see page 214) (cut with a hot, wet knife and once cut immediately refrozen for at least 1 hour before wrapping)

1 litre rapeseed oil, for deep-frying

For the boozy shochu cherries

300g ripe cherries, washed, stems removed, roughly pounded in a mortar and stones removed

1 litre shochu (rice-based is my preference)

200ml cherry brandy

4 star anise

1mm round slice of ginger

You'll need to start making the boozy shochu cherries a good 11–12 days in advance, so plan well ahead. I suggest making a full batch – it's more than you'll need for this recipe but you'll be thankful (or not) when you see these little fuckers winking at you from their jar when you stand staring into your fridge.

Mix the cherries into the shochu and decant into a Kilner jar or similar. Allow to sit in a fairly cool room for 10 days – this is really important, it needs to be a cool room! Chill in the fridge until needed.

In a saucepan, combine the strained shochu, cherry brandy, star anise and ginger and bring to the boil. Reduce the heat. Using the point of a skewer, make about 10 small holes in each cherry.

Drop the cherries into the hot liquid and cook for 25 minutes. Remove from the heat and allow to cool down, then chill in an airtight jar. Keep refrigerated for a day or so before use.

On the day you want to serve, cut 4 triangular shapes from the pastry, edges about 15cm each, and set aside.

Mix the tempura flour with just a little water and whisk until you have a semi-thick paste. Brush your first triangle all over with the flour mix. Take an iced parfait log from the freezer; place it 1.5cm from the bottom of the pastry and roll it up towards the point of the triangle. Press the pastry at either end to ensure the parfait is sealed.

Brush a little more flour mix on the tip of the pastry to help secure it and freeze immediately. Repeat the process for the remaining 3 logs and pastry pieces.

After at least an hour or so, and when you're ready to serve, heat the super-clean oil in a fryer or large pan to 180°C/350°F. Once hot, take the parfait logs straight from the freezer and fry for about 1½ minutes, until golden.

Strain off some of the juices from the cherries before serving with the fried parfait logs.

COLD SUSHI RICE AND YAKULT PUDDING

The Yakult happened to be in the right place at the right time and that was it - it was dumped into the chilled rice pudding and it was fucking great!

For those of you who don't know what Yakult is, firstly where the hell have you been? And secondly it is a fermented milk drink, which contains a load of probiotic bacteria which was named Lactobacillus Casei Shirota, after the Japanese scientist, Minoru Shirota, who created it.

You can top this with whatever takes your fancy. Here, I have used the boozy shochu cherries (see page 221) and some pistachios, but you might also want to try it with coconut ice cream, yuzu custard or whisky-soaked raisins.

SERVES 6

125g salted butter
150g caster sugar
200g sushi rice
1.8 litres milk
300ml double cream
4–6 × 65ml bottles Yakult

To serve
18 boozy shochu cherries (see page 222)
a few pistachios, lightly crushed

Preheat the oven the 110°C/90°C fan/Gas Mark ¼.

Melt the butter and sugar in a saucepan over a medium-high heat, stirring occasionally until it turns golden brown.

Add the rice, stir well until completely combined and the rice is well coated, and then pour in the milk and cream. This will immediately cause the caramel to harden – this is normal and it will melt.

Bring the mix to the boil and then pour into a 3-litre capacity casserole dish, cover with parchment paper and place into the preheated oven. Bake for approximately 1½ hours, until thick and creamy.

Allow the rice pudding to cool down and then chill. Give it a good hour or so in the fridge before you stir though the Yakult. The trick is to add the Yakult right before serving so that it doesn't get absorbed by the rice and thicken again slightly, which is what will happen if you do it too far in advance. I like my rice pudding to have quite a wet texture so I'd go for adding all 6 bottles. If you're not so sure, add 4 and see how you like the taste and texture.

Top with the boozy shochu cherries and pistachios, or whatever your topping of choice is.

DRINKING

APPLE, LIME AND JASMINE INFUSION

Iced teas are my drink of choice - if I'm off the hard stuff! I'd never really been into iced tea until I moved to France. Lipton lemon or peach flavours were everywhere, and even though it was freezing cold (I was in Chamonix), iced tea was the quencher of choice: watery enough to quench, sweet enough to make you feel half alive again after a big night out.

This version hails from an overindulgent period when I lived in Dubai; me and my mate, who was known as Pavlè Foreman (you know who you are), used to eat so much fucking food we both become seriously fat (it's what happens when bars open until 2am and burger-delivery guys are out all night). Anyway, we came across something like this version one afternoon whilst smashing dumplings, Kung Fu Panda style. We finally escaped the dust, the heat, the touchy police (that's a different story...) and got to work on a new menu in a new town in the UK. We came up with this. It's an all-round ripper. Use it as a quencher, top it off with ice-cold vodka, make a sorbet or do little apple cups and cleanse your diners' palates.

SERVES 4-6

For the tea infusion
40g jasmine tea leaves
500ml cold filtered water

For the lime and lemongrass syrup
500g caster sugar
6 lemongrass stalks, bruised with the blunt end of a knife
a small handful of lime leaves (must be fresh, or use frozen – dried are rubbish)

For the base mix
500g run-of-the-mill apple juice
125ml filtered water

First make the tea infusion. Infuse the jasmine tea in the water and refrigerate for 8 hours. Strain.

Make the syrup by heating the sugar, lemongrass stalks, lime leaves and 500ml of water until the sugar dissolves. Take off the heat and leave to cool, and then store in the fridge overnight. Strain before use.

Combine the chilled tea infusion and syrup with the apple juice and water and mix well. Chill before use and serve over ice, when appropriate. This will keep in the fridge for about a week or so.

Oven temperatures

°C	°C Fan	Gas Mark	°F
110°C	90°C Fan	Gas Mark ¼	225°F
120°C	100°C Fan	Gas Mark ½	250°F
140°C	120°C Fan	Gas Mark 1	275°F
150°C	130°C Fan	Gas Mark 2	300°F
160°C	140°C Fan	Gas Mark 3	325°F
180°C	160°C Fan	Gas Mark 4	350°F
190°C	170°C Fan	Gas Mark 5	375°F
200°C	180°C Fan	Gas Mark 6	400°F
220°C	200°C Fan	Gas Mark 7	425°F
230°C	210°C Fan	Gas Mark 8	450°F
240°C	220°C Fan	Gas Mark 9	475°F

Useful conversions

1 tablespoon = 3 teaspoons
1 level tablespoon = approx. 15g or ½oz
1 heaped tablespoon = approx. 30g or 1oz
1 egg = 55ml / 55g / 1fl oz

INDEX

F

Fire Pit Quail 103

fish

    BBQ skate with soba vinaigrette 177

    butter fried Dover sole 174

    Chilean sea bass 123

    chirashi sushi bites 159

    see also eel; salmon; seafood; tuna; yellowtail

Flamed Edamame with Butter, Lemon and Sea Salt 16

Flamed Scallop Sashimi with Kimchi Butter and Tobiko 38

foie gras

    kobu-jime with salmon 57

    nigiri 152

    unagi with apple balsamic 170

Fried Cashews with Dried Miso, Lime and Chilli 20

Fried Chicken Maki with Umami Mayo and Chilli Ponzu 144

Fried Chicken Party 74

Fried Raspberry Ice Cream 'Harumaki' with Boozy Shochu Cherries 222

fries sweet potato and soba 23

fruit

    banana cream pie 208

    boozy shochu cherries 222

    caramelised apricots 218

    grapefruit with razor clam salad 49

    lychee shochu shot 239

    passion fruit and sake parfait 217

    watermelon with crispy skin duck 181

    see also apples; raspberries; yuzu

G

Gen Mai Cha Soft Serve in Sesame Ice Cream Cones 211

Goba Tempura with Kinome Salt and Grapes 78

Grains and Greens Salad with Honey, Soy and Ginger Dressing 53

grapefruit razor clam salad 49

green tea

    gen mai cha ice cream 211

    iced matcha latte 231

gyoza smokey pork with sesame dip 186

H

Hijiki Salad 41

hoba leaf with mushrooms 198

Hot Sauna Poussin 197

I

ice cream

    fried raspberry 'harumaki' 222

    gen mai cha 211

    sake kasu 208

    soba 218

Iced Matcha Latte 231

Iced Passion Fruit and Sake Parfait 217

Iced Raspberry Parfait with Black Sugar Syrup 214

Iced Sweet and Sour Nasu 46

N

nanban zuke 247

Nika Whisky Espresso Martini 235

noodles chilled somen with shiitake broth 50

nuts

cashew with miso, lime and chilli 20

peanut soy 181

O

offal

chicken liver parfait 141

see also foie gras

Okonomiyaki — Kurobuta Style 178

onions crunchy rings 67

Onsen Eggs with Truffle Salt 194

oysters cream 57

P

Pan-Fried Duck Roll 162

pancakes

okonomiyaki 178

soba with crab and yuzu kosho 45

passion fruit iced parfait with sake 217

peanuts soy 181

Pickled Langoustine Nigiri with Green Chilli 148

pickles

cucumber 248

kimchi 246

ponzu sauce 247

pork

barbecued ribs with honey, soy and ginger glaze 63

buta no kakuni with mustard 165

marbou dofu 166

slow-cooked belly with miso 107

smokey gyoza with sesame dip 186

tea-smoked scratchings 27

see also bacon

potatoes

mountain buns with rabbit 173

truffle dip 12

see also sweet potatoes

poultry *see* chicken; duck; quail

prawns

shrimp tempura with kimchi 81

teapot soup 202

puffed soba 248

Pumpkin Tempura 89

Q

quail fire pit 103

R

rabbit miso yaki with potato buns 173

raspberries

fried ice cream 'harumaki' 222

iced parfait 214

Razor Clam Salad with Grapefruit and Tosazu 49

ABOUT THE AUTHOR

Born in Collie, Western Australia, Scott Hallsworth left school at 16 to take up an apprenticeship as a chef, and has never looked back (other than wanting to be in a rock 'n' roll band).

He worked across the world until joining Nobu London in 2001 as a Chef de Partie. He went on to spend six years at the Michelin-starred Park Lane address where he was promoted to Head Chef. In 2007 he moved to Australia to open Nobu Melbourne, before moving to Dubai to help open Mirai restaurant.

In 2013, Scott began devising the Kurobuta concept and opened the doors of the first Kurobuta pop up that same year. There are now two London locations.

MUSICAL INFLUENCES IN MY FOOD

If you really want to get into the groove when eating or cooking the recipes in this book, try making a mix tape with some of my favourites:

PAVEMENT
PIXIES
THE GO BETWEENS
SILVER JEWS
CRAIG HALLSWORTH (MY BRO!)
BEST COAST
BILLY BRAGG
THE NATIONAL
YOU AM I
INTERPOL
THE LEMONHEADS
NICK CAVE AND TBS
BEIRUT
PJ HARVEY
PAUL KELLY
COURTNEY BARNETT
SONIC YOUTH

ACKNOWLEDGEMENTS

The amazing crew of Kurobuta, past and present - especially the chefs who ran around like maniacs when we were shooting the photos, namely Mark Morrans and Eneko Canovas.

Ben Liebmann for instigating this book and for being one of the few who supported the early Kurobuta playlists.

David and Ange Loftus for such great photo shoots and a load of laughs!

To my mum, dad, Ken, Craig and family, Goz and family for the years and years of support and encouragement.

Finally a big thanks to Phar for all of your help, support and trying to kick my ass to write so many times!

Publisher Jon Croft
Commissioning Editor Meg Avent
Projects Editor Emily North
Designers Kim Musgrove and Marie O'Mara
Art Director Kim Musgrove
Photographer David Loftus
Props Stylist Ange Loftus
Copy editor Kate Wanwimolruk
Proofreader Margaret Haynes
Home Economist Elaine Byfield
Indexer Zoe Ross

Absolute Press
An imprint of Bloomsbury Publishing Plc

50 Bedford Square	1385 Broadway
London	New York
WC1B 3DP	NY 10018
UK	USA

www.bloomsbury.com

ABSOLUTE PRESS and the A. logo are trademarks of
Bloomsbury Publishing Plc

First published 2017

© Scott Hallsworth, 2017
Photography © David Loftus, 2017

British Library Cataloguing-in-Publication Data
A catalogue record for this book is available from the British
Library.

Library of Congress Cataloguing-in-Publication data has been
applied for.

ISBN: HB: 9781472919922
ePDF: 9781472919939
ePub: 9781472919946

2 4 6 8 10 9 7 5 3 1

Printed and bound in China by C&C Offset Printing Co.

Bloomsbury Publishing Plc makes every effort to ensure
that the papers used in the manufacture of our books are
natural, recyclable products made from wood grown in well-
managed forests. Our manufacturing processes conform to the
environmental regulations of the country of origin.

To find out more about our authors and books visit
www.bloomsbury.com. Here you will find extracts, author
interviews, details of forthcoming events and the option to sign up
for our newsletters.